John Plunket Joly and the Great Famine in King's County

Maynooth Studies in Local History

SERIES EDITOR Raymond Gillespie

This year, Maynooth Studies in Local History publishes its 100th study. Over the twenty years of the series these short books have ranged widely, both chronologically and geographically, over the local experience in the Irish past. They have demonstrated the vitality of the study of local history in Ireland and have shown the range of possibilities open to anyone interested in studying local history. From medieval Dalkey to Granard in the 1950s, past volumes in this series have dissected the local experience in the complex and contested social worlds of which it is part. Perhaps inevitably, many have concentrated on well-established paths of enquiry with works on the Famine of the 1840s and the late 19th-century land war, while others reveal the riches that await gathering from the medieval and early modern worlds. The sister series, Maynooth Research Guides in Local History, has also facilitated access to these worlds by providing reliable and user-friendly resources that help those unfamiliar with the raw evidence to deal with the sometimes difficult sources that survive from the more remote past. Studies of local worlds over such long periods are vital for the future since they not only stretch the historical imagination but provide a longer perspective on the evolution of local societies in Ireland and help us to understand more fully the complex evolution of the Irish experience. The existence of a large body of published studies, which are not a simple chronicling of events relating to an area within administrative or geographically determined boundaries, opens the possibility of comparative study to allow us to see better why particular regions had their own personality in the past. Such an exercise is clearly one of the most exciting challenges for the future.

Like previous volumes in the series, the six short books published as part of this centenary offering are reconstructions of the socially diverse worlds of the poor as well as the rich, women as well as men, and reconstruct the way in which those who inhabited those worlds lived their daily lives, often little affected by the large themes that dominate the writing of national history. In addressing these issues, studies such as those presented in these short books, are at the forefront of Irish historical research and represent some of the most innovative and exciting work being undertaken in Irish history today. They also provide models that others can follow up and adapt in their own studies of the Irish past. In such ways will we understand better the regional diversity of Ireland and the social and cultural basis for that diversity. These books convey the vibrancy and excitement of the world of Irish local history today.

Maynooth Studies in Local History: Number 103

John Plunket Joly and the Great Famine in King's County

Ciarán Reilly

FOUR COURTS PRESS

Set in 10pt on 12pt Bembo by
Carrigboy Typesetting Services for
FOUR COURTS PRESS LTD
7 Malpas Street, Dublin 8, Ireland
www.fourcourtspress.ie
and in North America for
FOUR COURTS PRESS
c/o ISBS, 920 N.E. 58th Avenue, Suite 300, Portland, OR 97213.

ISBN 978-1-84682-355-8

Printed in England by
Antony Rowe Ltd, Chippenham, Wilts.

Contents

Acknowledgments

I wish to first thank Dr Terence Dooley for his continued guidance. Professor Mary Ann Lyons, Head of the Department of History, NUI Maynooth, has been particularly supportive of my postdoctoral research; I thank her sincerely. I also offer thanks to her predecessor, Professor R.V. Comerford and to Professor Raymond Gillespie for the kind invitation to be part of this series. It is a great pleasure to acknowledge the assistance and support that the Offaly Historical & Archaeological Society has given in regard to the Joly diaries; in particular, I thank Michael Byrne, Stephen McNeill and John Kearney. Similar thanks is expressed to my colleagues at the Centre for the Study of Historic Irish Houses & Estates; the staff of the John Paul II Library, NUI Maynooth; the Russell Library, NUI Maynooth; the National Library of Ireland; the Representative Church Body Library of Ireland; Trinity College Library; the National Archives of Ireland and the St Kevin's Parish Vestry, Clonbullogue. I wish also to thank my parents and family for their continued friendship. Finally, this book is dedicated to my wife Tara for her unstinting support and love.

Introduction

'That year is all over, a good one it was, that the next may be as good'.[1] Writing in his diary on 1 January 1847, John Plunket Joly (1826–58) of Hollywood House, near Bracknagh, King's County (Offaly), brings to an end the year 1846, almost 15 months after the arrival of the potato blight in Ireland. Such a description of life in King's County during the Great Famine is in stark contrast to the almost daily pleas of suffering from the poor and dying. For example, at nearby Edenderry the Revd James Colgan remarked that the 'potatoes are now almost entirely exhausted' and that 'families are in a pitiable condition'.[2] The workhouse at Edenderry, originally built to accommodate 600 people, housed three times as many, while the Board of Guardians petitioned government for help as 'distress daily increases among all classes of the poor'.[3] Indeed a contemporary writer, William Wilde, remarked of the area that 'there must be something wrong in the system which produces all this misery in the neighbourhood of such a fertile country'.[4] Such was the extent of the calamity in King's County that during the period under study, 1845–51, the population declined by 23 per cent, or 34,000 people. Although other areas saw a greater decrease in population, it has been argued that 'the crisis caused by crop failure in Offaly in the late 1840s had proportionally a greater impact than in some of the western counties'.[5]

While many works have been published about the Great Famine, particularly during the sesquicentenary commemoration in the mid-1990s, few have examined areas which were not as adversely affected by the calamity. Most Famine studies (if not all) highlight poverty, distress, disease, death, eviction and emigration. Few, if any, highlight the normality of life for some. For John Plunket Joly and his family, it appears life was undisturbed by the Famine. Daily activities such as music and dancing remained constant features of their social world as did farming duties including the making of hay, sheep shearing and the gathering of the harvest. Joly's diaries provide a daily account of life in King's County and offer a unique insight into aspects of what can be best described as a hidden Ireland during the Famine. Other Famine accounts are usually told through the eyes of travel writers, often detached from rural communities, such as James Hack Tuke, Asenath Nicholson and the Halls and, with the exception of the oft-quoted Mrs Smith of Baltiboys, Co. Wicklow, there are few first-hand accounts from people who actually lived through the Famine. This dearth of Famine related diaries and correspondence highlights the importance of the Joly archive.

The Joly diaries, located in the National Library of Ireland and Trinity College Dublin, cover the periods 1843 to 1848 and 1851 to 1858. These latter years are marked by Joly's appointment to the rectory of Clonsast (when he succeeded his father) and also his marriage to Julia Anna, daughter of Frederick, Count Lusi. Diaries for the period 1849 to 1850 do not survive, coinciding with the period that Joly spent in England training to be ordained. In addition to these, a smaller diary covering the period July to August 1846, records the travels of the Joly brothers to Belgium.[6] One of the most interesting aspects of the diaries are the numerous and almost daily sketches that accompany the text, and on occasion speak louder than the words. These sketches illuminate the social world of 19th-century Ireland, providing images of daily customs, practice, social and leisure pursuits. The diaries contain frequent entries as to the purchase of books and thus it was little wonder that when his brother, Jasper Robert, donated over 23,000 volumes in the 1870s, it was the largest collection ever deposited in the National Library.[7] When these diaries are used in conjunction with other primary source material, they help illuminate the local community and world in which the family resided.

For the purpose of this study, the diaries were supplemented by local and national newspapers, estate papers, outrage papers, relief commission papers and parliamentary reports. An insight into the travails of pre-Famine Clonsast, where the Jolys resided, is provided in the *Royal commission on the condition of poorer classes in Ireland* or, as it is more commonly known, the Poor Inquiry of 1835. Likewise, the Clonsast parish vestry minutes in the Representative Church Body Library elucidate on the local landscape, as do the parish records of births, marriages and deaths. In addition several estate and personal papers were consulted, including those relating to the Downshire, Ashtown, Rosse, Ponsonby and Ridgeway estates. The rich and varied folklore of the parish also informs this study. To date, only Patrick Henchy has examined the Joly family in any detail.[8]

In 1973, The friends of the National Library, under the then director, Patrick Henchy, placed an inscription over the headstone of Jasper Robert Joly (1819–92) in St Kevin's, Church of Ireland at Clonbullogue, Co. Offaly.[9] On the occasion Henchy described Joly as 'the greatest collector who ever lived in Ireland of books, drawings, prints and manuscripts'.[10] He also noted that for some of the National Library staff, the churchyard at Clonbullogue, where the Joly family are interred, had become a place of pilgrimage.[11] In 1816 the family settled in King's County when the Revd Dr Henry Joly (1784–1852) was granted the rectory of Clonsast by Augustas Frederick Fitzgerald, 3rd duke of Leinster. The position of rector was more than likely a result of his father's long service to the Leinster family. However, speaking of such associations were discouraged by Jean Jasper Joly, who in the last years of life warned his son: 'never mention your ancestry (except to your son) for even if you attain a middle class situation you will always be regarded as the son of the valet to the duke of Leinster and you will expose yourself to the ridicule of great and small alike'.[12]

The Jolys originated in Burgundy and other areas of France and Belgium and the family lineage can be traced to 1380. Jean Jasper Joly was born on 8 February 1740 in Charneux in the diocese of Liege, in modern day Belgium. In January 1756 as a citizen of Hungary and Bohemia he was issued a passport 'to travel far and wide without disruption'. The passport noted that 'he journeys from time to time in the towns and country districts lying around us, sometimes with a companion known to him, by the mercy of God free from all contagious diseases and making profession of the Catholic Apostolic Faith'.[13] In July 1770, leaving Brussels to be a 'voyageur', Joly spent several years in the service of an English merchant, John Osborne. With him he travelled throughout Europe and allegedly had an audience with Pope Clement XIII in April 1767. In July 1768 he entered into the employment of William Robert FitzGerald, marquess of Kildare and later 2nd duke of Leinster, who was undertaking his grand tour of the Continent. The family historian has suggested that Joly gave the young peer a loan of £1,000 and as a result was employed as Kildare's private secretary. Together they travelled across Europe visiting, among other places, Milan, Venice, Dresden and Berlin before eventually reaching Ireland on 5 October 1769.

Quickly settling into life in Ireland and his new role as private secretary, Jean Jasper became a Freeman of Dublin City in 1774, married Mary Rumley of Aghadda, Co. Cork and converted to Protestantism later that year.[14] Whether or not this conversion was a requirement of FitzGeralds, who had succeeded to the dukedom the previous year on the death of his father James (1722–73), is unclear. Certainly his promotion to the position of doorkeeper of the Irish House of Lords in June 1775 had much to do with Leinster's influence. This position was a sinecured post, coming with a £100 annual salary and also brought Joly into higher social circles: 'Jasper Joly has been recommended to me as a sober, faithful, diligent person, a Protestant and one very capable of performing the duty and service of a doorkeeper'.[15] Joly is credited with the rescue of two tapestries when the House of Lords went on fire on 27 February 1792. These tapestries, 'The valiant defence of Londonderry' and 'The glorious battle and victory of the Boyne', were made by John Van Beaver in 1732. In reward for his bravery he was presented with a copy of both tapestries in oils by James Mahony. Joly continued to serve the duke of Leinster and was featured in the famous Wheatley painting of the Irish Volunteers on College Green on 4 November 1779. Joly is depicted standing directly behind the duke of Leinster.[16] In 1793 he applied for naturalization papers and was later appointed as 3rd lieutenant of the 1st Company Stephen's Green Infantry during the 1798 rebellion.[17] This position is particualry interesting in light of the role of Lord Edward FitzGerald (1763–98), a United Irishman and brother of the duke of Leinster who was killed on 23 May 1798. It has been suggested that Lord Edward was shielded from English soldiers during the rebellion by Joly at Harcourt Terrace.[18] It was here that Joly first began to invest in property, building several houses, and he later took out mortgages on numbers 10, 11, 12 and 13 Charlemont Place. A four-acre field at the rear of Harcourt Terrace was known as 'Joly's field'. By the time of his death in 1824, Jean Jasper Joly owned 19 houses in Dublin and had established himself among the city's entrepreneurial class.

His son, Henry Edward, was born in December 1784 and baptized in Leinster House where his godparents, Lord Edward and Lady Emily FitzGerald, were present. He was educated privately by a tutor called Newland and entered Trinity College in 1797, obtaining a BA in 1801, an MA in 1810 and an MD from Dublin University in 1812. While a student at Trinity College he was also employed as a tutor to the children of the duke of Leinster and his diaries contain an interesting account of life at Carton during the years 1801 to 1803. In 1813 Henry Joly married Martha Revell from Co. Wicklow and three years later was appointed to the rectory of Clonsast. Together they had four children: Jasper Robert (1823–92); Henry Charles (1825–91); John Plunket (1826–58) and Mary (1830–51). He was later chancellor of Kildare (1849–52) and archdeacon of Killala (1850–2). By comparison with his patron, the duke of Leinster, Joly's holding in King's County was particularly small. On the eve of the Famine the family's estate consisted of 1,363 acres, located in the townlands of Kilcloncorkey (244 acres), Clonbullogue (522 acres) and Bracknagh (597 acres). (By the 1870s it amounted to just over 2,500 acres.) Joly also acquired over 1,500 acres at Carrigaholt, a remote part of south Co. Clare, in the barony of Moyarta, which he purchased for £11,000 from Lord William FitzGerald in 1835.[19] Although relatively small landlords, the Jolys enjoyed considerable social status in Clonsast as the principal resident landlords in the parish.

1. Pre-Famine landscape and community

The parish of Clonsast, which translates as 'the field of rough grass', is located in the north-east of Offaly, in the barony of Coolestown, close to where the three counties of Offaly, Laois (formerly Queen's County) and Kildare meet. At the heart of the parish of Clonsast is the village of Clonbullogue, some 6 miles from Portarlington in Laois, 11 miles from Daingean (formerly Philipstown), 5 miles from Edenderry and 6 miles from Rathangan in Co. Kildare. In the distance, the hill of Allen is a firm reminder of the region's geologic formation. In his *Statistical survey of King's County* published in 1801, Sir Charles Coote noted that half of the barony of Coolestown was bog and waste.[1] However, he did concede that 'the country abounds with a fine rich grass and only wants draining and gravelling to be made of the very best quality'.[2] On the eve of the Famine, Clonsast had 3,914 inhabitants and comprised over 25,000 statute acres, of which about 14,000 were deemed to be cultivable, the remainder bog. An area known as the 'great bog of Clonsast' was over 8,000 acres and measured 20 feet deep in parts. Indeed, when Bord na Mona was established in the 1940s, Clonsast was among the first of the bogs in Ireland to be developed.[3] Throughout the 1830s much of the parish underwent reclamation projects to drain the land, but an 1846 estimate concluded that it would cost £12,695 to salvage the remaining portion of bog. The area was also noted for its high deposits of gravel located at Tooreen, Kylebeg and Enaghan.[4]

Extending eight miles from north to south and six miles from east to west (from Rathangan to Walsh Island), Clonsast is located in what was formerly known as upper Tethmoy, Tuath dhá Mhuige, or the upper land of two plains.[5] In his survey of Offaly's townlands and parishes, Thomas Lee notes that the parish has few evident archaeological remains, something he found surprizing given the size of the parish.[6] However, Bronze Age settlements have been located in Clonsast, one of the very few in modern Co. Offaly.[7] Located on the Figile river, a tributary of the River Barrow, Clonsast was said to have been the location of the ancient wood of Leinster, Fidh Gaibhle, from which, legend states, Brian Boru selected timber to construct boats in preparation for the Battle of Clontarf in 1014.[8] In addition, the great Book of Clonsast, now said to be lost and predicting the coming of the Vikings and others to Ireland, was written in the locality in the 7th century.[9] According to the Revd Martin Comerford, historian of the diocese, this book, also known as 'Leabhar Cluana Sost', is recorded in the contents of the 'Leabhar Breac', or speckled book and was the work of St Brochan who flourished in the seventh century.[10] When compiling his work for the Ordnance Survey of Ireland in the late 1830s, John O'Donovan noted that Clonsast was 'a beautiful cluain which is surrounded by a part of the Bog of Allen'. He further added that: 'the Irish name is Cluain Sosta (Sasta) and the patron is vividly remembered to be St Brachan (Brochan?) (Perhaps a contraction for Berachan) whose memory was annually celebrated with great devotion at his well called Tobar-Brachain on the third of December'.[11] According to Elizabeth FitzPatrick, Cluain Sosta was one of the most celebrated monasteries in Uí Failghe.[12] St Berchan, or Broughan, is described in the 'Felire Oengusso' as 'Fer da leth', the man of two parts, who spent half of his life 'in the world' and the other half on pilgrimage, where he was said to have travelled between Ireland and Scotland.[13] Writing in the 'Leabhar Breac', MacEgan, a scribe, contends that the 'Book of Berchan' was housed at Clonsast until at least the 16th century. He writes: 'May eve this day in Cluain Sosta Berchan, I am in it writing the conclusion of this story [i.e. of Alexander], firstly from the Book of Berchan of the Cluain'.[14] The monastery was located on an island of dry land surrounded by the Bog of Allen. The 'Martyrology of Donegal' describes St Brochan as one of the four great prophets of Erin.[15] Significantly for this study, the site of the monastery was a place of pilgrimage during Famine times and indeed for the Joly family.

The parish of Clonsast was variously named over the years; in the 14th century it was part of the territory of the Clann Maol Ughra or Clanmaliere (the land of the O'Dempseys). On Cotton's 1563 map of Laois and Offaly it was named Farranomurrighan or O'Murrigan's land.[16] By 1666 it was owned by Col. William Purefoy, a Cromwellian adventurer; thus the area became known as 'Purefoy's place'.[17] A massacre at Ballinowlarth in 1643 during the Confederate Wars greatly reduced the local population. On Little Christmas morning the Roman Catholic Church was surrounded, the doors locked and the congregation burned.[18] (In 1976 a commemorative mass was celebrated on the site after earlier excavations in 1917 had uncovered the skeletal remains of those who perished in the incident.)[19] By 1789 the village of Clonbullogue was the centre of social and commercial life in the parish and was described by the *Hibernian Gazetteer* as: 'Purefoy's place a fair town in King's County, 45 miles from Dublin. The fair day is on the 10 July. Millgrove is a pleasant seat on the banks of the Violet River'.[20] The village was subsequently destroyed during the 1798 rebellion, although the Ridgeways of Ballydermot were influential in the capture of Wexford rebels, the Revd Mogue Kearns and Colonel Anthony Perry, in July 1798 near Clonbullogue; they were later executed at nearby Edenderry. The location of their arrest, the 'wheelabout', is still known as the 'priest's bush' and said to have a cure for headaches.[21] Three years later Coote stated that there was a new church in the village, but that the houses were small and poor, while another village in the parish, Ballynure, was described as being 'very mean'.[22] Conditions had improved somewhat by the early 1830s when James Doyle, bishop of Kildare and Leighlin (1786–1834), on a confirmation visit to the parish, complimented the people of Bracknagh as some of the finest he had ever seen.[23]

The Joly estate was centred on the townlands of Clonbullogue, Clongarrett and Kilcloncorkey. Among the neighbouring landowners were minor gentry such as the Smiths, Nelsons and Ridgeways; and larger landowners such as Charles Manners St George, Lord Ashtown, Lord Downshire, Lord Rosse, Lord Digby and Lord Ponsonby. The duke of Leinster also owned a small estate near Rathangan which bordered with the Jolys. The parish also had a considerable number of large farmers of more than 500 acres such as the Goodwins, the Watsons and Humes in Cloncrane. There were also a number of absentee proprietors holding small pockets of land close to the village of Clonbullogue, including Captain Steele, Captain Rice, Captain Saunders and Robert Fitzgerald.[24]

The population of King's County, in line with the national growth, increased from 131,000 people in 1821 to just over 147,000 between 1831 and 1841.[25] Thus in less than three decades the population had increased by 27 per cent. The population of Clonsast rose from 2,914 people in 1831 to 3,803 10 years later, an increase of 31 per cent. The average holding in the county was five to 15 acres. In 1824 there were 637 inhabited houses in Clonsast, consisting of 687 families (1,947 males and 1,891 females), an average of six people per house.[26] On the eve of the Famine, chronic subdivision of land created numerous social problems. On the 14,000 acre Downshire estate at Edenderry (and which also included part of the village of Clonbullogue) subdivision caused such confusion that it was impossible to know which tenant held what land. In 1839, Downshire's agent, Thomas Murray, lamented that 'there are some cases where the people hold in common and have no regular divisions but lump together as say, two cows grass, three cows and two calves'.[27] Although many landlords or their agents spoke in favour of ending the practice of subdivision to the Devon Commission in 1844, few could do anything about it.

The rectory to which the Revd Henry Joly was appointed in 1816 was created in 1796 as part of the diocese of Kildare and together with the vicarage of Ballinakill formed the union of Clonsast, under the alternate patronage of the duke of Leinster and the bishop of Kildare.[28] In 1820 St Kevin's at Clonbullogue was described as a 'pretty good church' and much of its improvement was attributed to the exertions of the Revd Joly.[29] Social memory claims that the church, consecrated by Bishop Dopping of Kildare in 1681, was built from money left behind by a man who died in the area leaving gold in a boot. Thus the church was subsequently known as the 'boot of gold'. When renovated the church catered for 275 people, although the average attendance was estimated at under 100 people in the early 1840s. Throughout the Famine years numbers fell to as low as eight or nine attendants and indeed as late as 1853 the Revd John Plunket Joly lamented that the Easter Sunday service had attracted less than 30 people. In 1834, under the direction of his father, the Revd Henry Joly, the church was painted, the roof slated, a fence erected and walls erected around the perimeter.

In 1823 the Association for Promoting Christian Knowledge had established a school in Clonsast catering for 50 boys and girls.[30] A return of 1826 listed seven teachers working in the parish: John Cassidy at Clonsast, Daniel Connolly at Bracknagh, Mary Connor at Cloncashin, Richard Connor and Alicia McNamara at Clonbullogue, James Dunn at Millgrove and Francis Glanville at Clonmore. All except Glanville were Roman Catholics and were described as being 'young, of good character, the better instructed of our flock'.[31] There was also a noticeable increase in the numbers attending school before the Famine, which obviously increased after the introduction of the national education act in 1831. This rise in literacy levels was reflected in the success of the local Repeal clubs at Edenderry and Clonbullogue in the early 1840s where reading rooms and book clubs were established to expand the education of a new literate generation. The reading rooms were said to have been a huge success with the 'thirst for knowledge spreading among the people', and attracting a large number of ladies.[32]

In the late 18th century the completion of the Grand Canal (which entered King's County at nearby Edenderry and proceeded towards the River Shannon in the west) advanced the prosperity of the region by providing new and wider markets for agricultural produce. In 1801 some 110,855 tons of goods were shipped from Tullamore to Dublin along the Grand Canal; by 1845 that figure had increased to 280,000 tons.[33] However, when the Revd Henry Joly arrived in King's County in 1816, he found a distressed population, owing chiefly to the decline in fortunes of the woollen trade and other cottage industries at the end of the Napoleonic War. In 1760 the linen output of King's County had been estimated at £50,000 but had fallen to £20,000 in 1816. By 1839 there were only two mills in King's County, employing 56 people;[34] thus the smallholders of King's County who had previously supplemented their income through the linen industry witnessed a dramatic decline in their fortunes.[35] By 1841 almost 3 per cent of King's County families were living purely on charity or 'vested means'.[36]

In Clonsast the majority of the population depended on agriculture, mainly working small holdings. There were an estimated 82 people employed by various landowners.[37] Some were fortunate to be herds, 'a very comfortable class' who were allowed grass for one or two cows and were paid 10*d*. per week.[38] William Ridgeway of Ballydermot employed several herds, paying 'old Dowling to mind cattle for which he gets the entire of the garden and the use of one cow, his son Edward 10*d*. per day, Larry 8*d*. per day and Thomas and Mick 6*d*. per day'.[39] Sheep were important to the local economy, with Coote noting that one acre of land in Coolestown maintained five sheep, which was

1 Shearing sheep at Derrygarron as depicted in the Joly diaries.

called a collop.[40] Revd Joly also frequented the markets and fairs of Kildare, Rathangan, Mountmellick and Edenderry where he bought and sold his sheep and cattle. Edenderry was the main market town, but grain and other agricultural produce were also sent to Rathangan in Co. Kildare and Clonard in Co. Meath.[41] In 1845, Clonbullogue with its Church of Ireland church, inn, national school, blacksmith forge and Roman Catholic church was easily the centre of the parish. In the village and its vicinity lived a number of tradesmen such as: Samuel Crampton (wheelwright), Henry Crampton (brick maker), Florence Flynn (farrier), Thomas Crampton (baker), Richard Kelly (publican), Edward Finn (blacksmith), John Haughton (tailor) and Henry Justin (grocer).

In this predominantly rural community there was a reluctance to adopt new farming methods and practices among the farmers of Clonsast. Colonel Eamon Broy (1887–1972) later argued with some justification that 'the district is far off all beaten tracks, beside the great bog of Allen and so the people retained most of the ancient Irish characteristics and were to a certain extent unaffected by what is commonly referred to as progress'.[42] An insight into the pre-Famine farming practices of the barony of Coolestown is indicated in the correspondence of Henry Brereton, a land steward at the Ridgeway estate, who remarked, while visiting England in 1821, that 'these Englishmen are dammed queer fellows, they do not farm the way you do in the bogs, they sow nothing but clover, wheat and turnips'.[43] Moves to introduce new methods of farming were obstructed by the labouring classes who saw new technology as a threat to their livelihoods. At Rathmoyle, in the adjoining barony of Warrenstown, the noted Scottish agriculturalist George Kerr was repeatedly a target of assassination for his 'progressive farming' and for reducing the number of men employed on his farm. In 1831 William Cheyne, the son of a Dublin surgeon, was murdered at Rathmoyle when visiting the Kerrs.[44] At Walsh Island a plough was broken in 1838 in an attempt to promote employment among local labourers.[45] The breaking of a 'Scotch plough' at Capagolan was deemed further proof that some were reluctant to see change introduced in agriculture.[46] As one witness put it to the Poor Inquiry of 1835, many of the rural population were scared of change and saw the increased use of the plough as detrimental to their livelihoods.[47] Similarly, migrant workers were not welcomed in the area. In the 1830s Connacht men working in the barony of Clonlisk had their barrows broken to pieces.[48] In summation Clonsast on the eve of the Famine was something of a rural backwater where the people in general did not favour modernization. The area had not benefited to the same extent as Edenderry from the agricultural expansion of the Napoleonic era and in general the cottier tenants remained 'poor', surviving on a basic diet of potatoes and oat meal. Moreover, in the early decades of the 19th century there were severe outbreaks of cholera and typhus in 1817 and 1832 adding to their plight.[49] The general condition of the lower classes was summed up in the Poor Inquiry of 1835, which reported that 'the cottages of the peasants are miserably poor and wretched, in few instances weather proof; yet fondly clung to by the natives, who are attached to them by custom, and perhaps also from the warmth occasioned by their smoke and lowness'. Labourers were described as a 'wretched class and not better treated than slaves'.[50] Indeed, even the more wealthy farmers 'live well but are dirty' and 'they all refuse to live in slated houses, many of which have been erected by the gentry and are very ornamental to their demesnes, but are of no farther use, as they prefer clay huts'.[51]

In Clonsast, the Revd Joly concurred that poverty was exacerbated by such housing and noted that a large portion of the population clamoured to the cabins on the edges of the bog, which were 'wretched' and 'made of turf sods, extremely damp and poorly furnished'. This in turn led to disputes over turbary rights and the barony of Coolestown was particularly affected by such. One local landlord, Maunsell Dames, believed that 'the people fancy the bogs to be free property for all, and that often a man may find a house upon his bog in the morning where there was not a sign of such a thing the previous evening'.[52] Revd Newcomb of Clonsast believed that the diet of the lower orders was 'generally very poor', their clothing 'a very coarse description' and their bed clothes almost non-existent.[53] The parish vestry provided £2 annually to the poor to bury their dead. It also took charge of abandoned or orphaned children after 1831 when a committee, headed by John Ridgeway, was established. Anne Jenkinson was given £5 annually to maintain a 'foundling' who had been left at Derrymore in that year. Jenkinson, a nurse and friend of the Joly family, was still caring for the child in 1845. During the epidemic of cholera in the early 1830s, the vestry appointed Isaac Gatchell of Coolegagen, Thomas Smith of Ballyfore and William McMullin of Ballinakill to oversee the maintenance of a temporary dispensary and the whitewashing of houses.[54] However, not all in Clonsast were so poorly circumstanced. Charles Manners was particularly praising of his King's County tenants, near Clonbullogue in 1836 when he wrote:

> They were Flanagan a worthy, open hearted and mannered industrious quiet peasant, Shaugnessy his brother and Currie an excellent man but ill, Whelan the weaver a good creature and his brother also such, Duffy a well conducted smith and his lovely daughter of fifteen to whom I gave two shillings. We came on them quietly surprised and were astonished at the very unexpected cleanliness and neatness and order of their houses.[55]

Secret societies flourished in King's County and it was a noted hotbed of agrarian outrage. Revd Henry Joly was among a number of landowners in the barony of Coolestown who met on several occasions in the 1820s to quell disturbances and the rise in secret societies. In particular there had been a number of illegal gatherings in the barony under the pretext of football matches where men had been forced and beaten to join secret societies. As a means to put a stop to such activity, publicans were warned to close their premises at nine o'clock every evening while farmers were asked to dismiss any workers involved in such behaviour.[56] In 1834 several baronies in King's County were proclaimed. Two years later George Cornewall Lewis was informed that in King's County 'the character [of agrarianism] appeared to be resulting from a conspiracy to prevent any person from taking land, or from possessing land, from which the previous tenant had been ejected for rent, and threatening strangers of every description from coming into the country'.[57]

The Revd John Dunne of Clonbullogue believed that the 'unquiet' in the parish was generally a result of the tithes controversy. This was evidenced in 1832 when a large assembly, estimated at between 8,000 and 10,000 tithe payers, gathered at Clonbullogue in April to protest against the landlords of the area. The question of tithes had smouldered throughout the previous decade after a special meeting of the vestry in September 1823 fixed the payment of local tithes at £681 annually.[58] But the Revd Joly believed that the 'reform question' had led to unquiet in the parish and that 'many violent speeches and publications' had incited the inhabitants. This he believed was caused by 'interfering with vested rights, meddling with the setting of land, wages of labourers and even domestic arrangements'. He further reported that a 'savage murder besides some unsuccessful attempts at assassination' had taken place in the barony. Joly also condemned the over dependence on alcohol: 'whatever misery exists or corruption in morals, health and politics, may in a great measure be attributed to the use of ardent spirits whereof the consumption is immense'.[59] The use of such 'ardent spirits' was not helped by the presence of seven public houses in the parish, with illicit distillation also prevalent. This may have been why John O'Donovan noted in 1838 that the clergy of the area had recently put a stop to the holding of patterns or fairs in the locality owing to the violence that regularly ensued, the 'consequence of the bad effect of whiskey', and that they were hoping to have the men converted to the ways of Fr Matthew and his temperance movement.[60]

In the previous decades, there existed extreme religious paranoia surrounding the prophecies of Pastorini and the so-called 'Birr rebellion' of 1820, creating panic and fear that there existed a plot to murder the Protestant inhabitants of King's County.[61] A poem, 'Song for the 12th July 1843', written in King's County in 1843, further highlighted this divide and appealed for unity between the Protestant and Catholic inhabitants of the county: 'till then the orange lily be, thy badge, my patriotic brother, the everlasting green for me, and we for one another'.[62] There was also some evidence of religious tensions in the barony of Coolestown. A series of riots on 12 July 1841 in Edenderry prompted Lord Downshire to visit the estate in an effort to restore relations between his Protestant and Catholic tenants, noting that it was 'everyone's duty to obey laws and keep social order'.[63] It was suggested that the riots had occurred in Edenderry because it was the source of the River Boyne and was thus a 'Mecca' for Loyalists. Alexander Bingham was one of those who was involved in the riots in 1841 when ten Loyalists were arrested.[64] Although no charges were brought, the men, described as 'shabby genteel', were warned as to their future conduct. In 1844 a dispute between members of the Edenderry Temperance Band and Robert Bingham, a Protestant and a brother of the aforementioned Alexander, about the playing of music on the public road to Clonbullogue highlighted such tensions. In this instance Bingham accused members of the band, Thomas Rowland, Pat Byrne and Philip Kennedy, of playing tunes such as 'Patrick's Day'; 'Garryowen' and 'White Cockade' as they passed his house as a means of antagonizing him.[65]

As the Revd Joly suggested, the Repeal movement heightened local tensions. It was particularly strong in Clonsast and on the eve of the Famine, Repeal wardens, James Laughlin and Michael McGrattan, could count on a numerous and generous collection of the 'rent' in Clonbullogue and Bracknagh.[66] In December 1839, over £20 was collected in the barony (at a time when Lord Downshire provided £50 for the poor of the barony owing to a severe wet season when locals failed to save their turf).[67] The Repeal movement reached its height in 1843. In January 1843 William Connor of Walsh Island spoke at a well-attended Repeal meeting at Rahan where he condemned the payments of tithes, stating that it was a 'monstrous grievance to have to pay two clergy'. There was also anger expressed at the payment to 'dumb parishes', where the clergy had no one to preach to but still collected the tithes.[68] In July, local Repealers were informed that Daniel O'Connell would soon visit Tullamore and they were to have their subscriptions ready and present themselves 'twenty deep' at the demonstration.[69] In advance of O'Connell's visit another large Repeal meeting was held at Ballinagar, attracting crowds from Geashill, Edenderry, Philipstown, Kilclonfert and Clonbullogue. Appealing to his tenants at Edenderry and Clonbullogue, Lord Downshire lamented that 'the representation of the King's County is at present in the hands of the low Roman Catholic party and of the agitators'.[70] By 1843 it was obvious that social, religious and political tensions in the barony were reaching dangerous levels.

In May 1843 the murder of John Gatchell was something of a cause célèbre in the locality and epitomized the social problems which existed in King's County on the eve of the Famine. Gatchell was a justice of the peace and was employed as agent on the Garner estate at Aghameelick where there were long-standing arrears of rent.[71] He was shot returning from Edenderry where he had applied for notices to be served on several tenants.[72] Another report suggested that he was murdered returning from the home of Revd Ridgeway of Ballydermot, agent on the Hume estate, where he had been dining and that 'his ribs were beaten in completely, his throat cut and his body mangled in a shocking manner'.[73] In the Gatchell family history it simply states that he was 'killed in the land war'.[74] What is of particular relevance to this study is that the murder took place in the immediate world of the Joly family. The murder and trial caused a sensation in the barony and news of its proceedings occupied daily talk for many months afterwards. Rather surprisingly then, given the family's involvement in the case, John Plunket Joly in his personal diary simply notes 'John Gatchell, shot on the road from Clonad opposite Clonkan' and provides no further commentary on the murder. Lord Rosse charged an inquiry into the murder and among those present at Philipstown was Jasper Robert Joly.[75] In the house of commons Daniel O'Connell argued that Gatchell had been 'employed for some time past in turning out tenants from a property with which the management he was entrusted'. According to O'Connell: 'one family in particular had been driven from their home in a pitiless manner and had to take refuge under miserable sheeting', the agent had sold all their property and the tenants had contracted typhus fever.[76] This claim was later refuted by Jonathon Gatchell, a brother of the deceased.[77] The murder was a divisive issue among the local population of Clonsast. The magistrates 'experienced every difficulty with false swearing and fabricated stories'.[78] In addition, moral 'ostracization' was directed towards women in particular who gave evidence. When Alice Poole returned to Clonbullogue she was 'exposed to the persecution of the peasantry' as the locals refused to speak to her.[79] Another witness, Margaret Dunne, married a soldier while in protection and chose not to return to Clonsast.[80] Others allegedly left for America in the days and weeks after the murder.[81] Jasper Robert Joly was active in the inquiry and apprehension of Gatchell's alleged assassin; he informed the under secretary, Edward Lucas, that 'the lower classes in this neighbourhood are raising a subscription for the purpose of defending Thomas Dowling' the chief suspect who was a brother-in-law of the crown witness

James Dunn.[82] Joly was also responsible for the apprehension of other agrarian conspirators and a man named Hegarty who was arrested for selling seditious songs at this time.[83]

The murder of Gatchell was not an isolated incident; there were several other assassination attempts on landlords, agents and estate officials. In January 1839 Lord Norbury was murdered at his home at Durrow, while a year later an alleged plot was uncovered to shoot Lord Downshire at Edenderry.[84] On this occasion one man was heard to say that he would 'blow Downshire's brains out'.[85] This conspiracy supposedly resulted from a large eviction of tenants from the Downshire estate in the 1830s by the agent Thomas Murray, who is said to have delighted in clearing a 'cunning and knavish population'. According to Murray 'the persons I wish to get rid of are the poorer class of farmers or rather land holders who cannot get work for their families and eat up all that the land produces so that they never have a shilling in money to meet the rent day'.[86]

Thus on the eve of the Famine simmering discontent and the work of secret societies such as Rockites and Terryalts threatened the peace and stability of Clonsast. Assassination attempts, threatening letters, beatings, burning of crops and mutilation of animals were regular occurrences. It was even claimed that it was 'next impossible' to live in King's County without being sworn into a secret society.[87] In December 1844 it was reported that 'not a night passes without an outrage being committed in the county which bids fair to out rival – in deeds of blood and savage barbarity, neighbouring Tipperary'.[88] More often than not agrarian disputes were between smallholders and middlemen rather than between tenants and landlords. It has also been suggested that Ribbonism thrived in King's County owing to the influx of workers who were employed on the Grand Canal that traversed the county.[89] In 1843, in an effort to counteract the success of secret societies, Lord Downshire ordered that his tenants were not permitted to make or allow signal fires on the estate.[90] However, one of the problems with counteracting such disturbances was the failure of the local magistrates to meet. In April 1844, the Edenderry magistrates, of which Joly was a member, were reprimanded for not having held a petty sessions in the town in over three months.[91]

Remarkably, in his annual speech to the Parsonstown (Birr) Agricultural Society in 1843, Lord Rosse drew attention to the possibility of a future famine in Ireland:

> A year of scarcity will at length come, and with it, a visitation of the most awful famine, such as the history of the world affords very many examples of, a famine followed by pestilence, when the utmost exertion of the landlords of Ireland, of the government, and of the legislature, aided by the unbounded generosity of the people of England, would be totally inadequate to avert the most fearful calamities.[92]

However, he hardly expected that within such a period the calamity that he spoke about would arrive in King's County and the country as a whole.

In October 1845 Dr Richard Grattan and Edward Wolstenholme, chairman of the Edenderry board of guardians, argued there was not a single field in Kildare or King's County unaffected by the blight.[93] Later that month *The Times* reported that the 'rot is more or less extensive' throughout King's County.[94] At Philipstown, for instance, Joseph Grogan, Lord Ponsonby's agent, reported in the same month that:

> The crop is still in the fields in stacks and can't be got into the haggards as it is raining same every day and night and the corn has received some damage in the stacks. With regard to the potatoes at the first time I wrote to you there was not the least appearance of damage on them but at this moment there appears to be great damage to the potato crop in this county or any other part that I am in the habit of travelling along the canal line but it is damaged more or less and the people appears (sic) to be greatly alarmed on that account.[95]

The coming of the blight, as highlighted by Grogan, coincided with heavy flooding in many parts of the country thereby exacerbating the problem for farmers and labourers alike.[96] At Clonbullogue many fields were flooded and crops destroyed. By March 1846, a despondent Andrew Moore, clerk of the Edenderry Poor Law Union, wrote to the relief commissioners at Dublin Castle lamenting that he was 'fearful of the appearance and spread of fever in a maligned form, owing to the scarcity of food, and the great misery to be apprehended in the approaching season'.[97] His description was comparable to that of Revd James Colgan who wrote that at Edenderry 'there are very many poor housekeepers in this town and neighbourhood whose potatoes are now almost entirely exhausted' and that 'families are in a pitiable condition'.[98] Others like Thomas Byrne, the secretary of the union, appealed for Indian corn to be sent to Edenderry, while Michael Gilligan urged that soup kitchens be established.[99] At the Wakely estate in nearby Rhode, such was the scale of the widespread hunger that even the crows were alleged to have been reduced to skeletons.[1]

The early years of the Great Famine in King's County were characterized by haphazard attempts at relief by agents and landlords as they tried to come to terms with the deepening crisis. Typical of the hindrances to relief schemes was the petty squabbling in several parishes and baronies. This squabbling was essentially about boundaries and administration, on which landlords could not agree. At Geashill the Revd Wingfield Digby refused to raise funds for the baronies of Ballycowan and Kilcoursey and so set up his own relief committee in 1846. Likewise Henry Sheane set up a committee at Lusmagh to relieve the plight of over 1,000 starving tenants but the committee spilt from that at

Banagher over Lord Rosse's appointment as chairman.[2] In addition to these squabbles Lord Rosse, lord lieutenant of King's County, appears to have misinterpreted the reports that were sent to him, which included among others an informative account by Lord Charleville's agent Francis Berry. According to Berry a third of the potato crop was lost and he feared 'excitements if not disturbances' would result in further crop failures.[3]

Elsewhere in King's County the Revd J.P. Holmes of Ferbane warned that 'all the horrors of starvation will be experienced by half at least of the population' if relief was not immediately granted.[4] The Revd Henry Tyrrell, secretary of the Kinnitty relief committee, reported in October 1846 that destitution was widespread, potatoes were no longer available for human consumption and provisions were very dear: 'the people are remarkably quiet and patient', concluded Tyrrell.[5] A threatening notice posted at Philipstown in the same month warned that if the poor were not soon supplied with relief they would 'resort to harsh measures'.[6] By December many were reported to be surviving on boiled turnips and a little meal at Philipstown.[7] According to Francis Berry: 'the wretches would merely commit a crime to have themselves put in jail'.[8] Henry Sheane, agent on the Bell estate, reiterated this aversion to the workhouse; they would, he said, 'die in the ditch rather than go there'.[9] Less than a year after the first signs of blight, agents and landlords were accused of contributing to the misery of the people. Threatening letters posted throughout the county warned: 'Landlords use no tyranny, keep your trumpeters at home, tenants gather all your corn into your farmyards; also threaten agents, land jobbers, moneylenders and millers'.[10]

Many of the county's landed proprietors presumed that the blight was only a short-term problem. William O'Connor Morris, for example, later recalled that 'the memory of the distress of 1818–22 led many of the county's proprietors to believe that the failure of the potato crop would be short lived'. In his opinion this was 'not heartlessness but the dangerous ignorance of a class kept apart from the classes beneath it'.[11] Sometimes this was intentional: John Hussey Walsh noted with disappointment that there was an 'inability' or 'reluctance' of the landlords in the barony of Lower Philipstown to subscribe to relief efforts.[12] However, the real problem in King's County in 1845 was the scarcity of seed potatoes for the following season. Lord Rosse so despaired of the situation that he claimed little over six weeks of provisions remained in the county and he feared for the outcome.[13] This was confirmed when the amount of land under potatoes in King's County in 1846 fell by over 5,000 acres.[14]

At Edenderry, in the same year, on the motion of Richard More O'Ferrall, it was resolved to ask for permission to procure one or two houses in each electoral division for the provision of soup kitchens.[15] According to O'Ferrall £30 was sufficient to establish a soup kitchen. Meanwhile, Repeal money continued to be collected throughout the barony, although the Repealers in

Edenderry, which included several men with 'enlarged views', were reprimanded for their lack of action.[16] However, in January 1847 they opened a soup 'shop' giving relief to 47 families consisting of 156 persons.[17] The need to do so was highlighted at the Edenderry Petty Sessions in June 1847 when it was alleged that substandard Indian meal was being sold in the town.[18] In addition potato seed that had been given to tenants for planting was instead used for food.[19]

The journal of James Dillon, the county coroner, offers an insight into the social conditions of the time.[20] Dillon conducted well over a thousand inquests in King's County during the Famine, highlighting, for example, the number of people who committed suicide. According to Dillon's verdicts some fell into water 'casually' while others 'casually' fell into bog holes. In May 1846 Thomas Brien of Doon Cross died from the 'overuse of ardent spirits', but, of course, the vast majority succumbed to hunger, fever and cold. Dillon's journal includes accounts of the Famine dead in the immediate world of John Plunket Joly. On 23 August 1846, Dillon was present at Cushina where an inquest was carried out on the body of Michael Connell who had 'casually' drowned in the river; on the body of Sarah Cobbe at Clonsast in February 1847 who had died of apoplexy and at Edenderry where Charles Fitzgerald committed suicide by hanging himself from a tree, leaving behind a wife and five children.[21]

The employment of the poor on various relief works temporarily stemmed the tide of starvation. A report of October 1846 noted that there was 'little if any distress among the labouring classes at Edenderry owing to the employment on the board of works clearing fifteen miles on the [River] Boyne'.[22] Some like Dr Richard Grattan though believed that while drainage and other public works schemes were beneficial they were not the final solution to feeding the masses.[23] The numbers employed on relief projects in the county rose from 718 at the beginning of July 1846 to over 3,750 by the end of that month.[24] By the end of 1847 this number had escalated to 12,557.[25]

As the Famine years progressed the situation in King's County became particularly fraught. Two landlords, four land agents and three other estate employees were murdered between 1845 and 1852.[26] These crimes represented the most serious manifestation of the violence directed against land agents and others during these years. Had would-be assassins been better shots the figures might have been considerably higher. King's County ranked the ninth highest in Ireland in 1846 for the number of threatening letters that were sent, while in 1847 an average of eight robberies a day were reported in the county.[27] The county also had the highest number of evictions in Leinster as the decade came to a close. In 1849 some 619 families, numbering 3,255 individuals, were evicted in King's County.[28] Of these some 123 families (or 631 people) were later readmitted as caretaker tenants. Such was the level of eviction that the inhabitants of King's County presented a petition to the house of commons in 1849 to alter the law of landlord and tenant in Ireland.[29] However, a year later King's County again had the highest level of eviction in Leinster with 652 families' evicted numbering 3,346 people.[30]

The increased rate of eviction resulted from the changing attitude of landlords, agents and others in King's County. In many cases more than five years' rent was due and once lenient landlords and their agents began to press for arrears and to clear the land. In 1848 Persse Grome, a Parsonstown poor law guardian, told a meeting of the board that it was:

> truly ridiculous to be wasting so much of their valuable time in talking over so much unimportant matters. It was all sympathy for paupers, beggars and brats and in what way they were to be made comfortable, as they had not been used to cabins and hovels of the meanest and filthiest kind from their birth; such talk was really monstrous and absurd and while all the pity was for the beggars there was no sympathy for the landlords and gentlemen of the country, at whose expense these persons were to be fed sumptuously.

In conclusion he wished to hear no more of such talk.[31] Similarly, in May 1849, Dr Richard Grattan caused consternation and widespread condemnation when he informed the Dublin Central Relief Committee that the Edenderry board of guardians had passed a resolution in an effort to avert crowds of paupers inundating the town from Galway and other Famine stricken counties. In order to do so they had decided to transfer the paupers to Dublin. 'The people of Edenderry are determined not to have the frightful scenes of other places enacted there, of hundreds of corpses lying unburied on the roads and ditches and devoured by dogs' he concluded.[32]

If eviction and clearance were not bad enough, heavy frost and rain had a disastrous effect on the harvest in King's County in 1848 and 1849.[33] Disease became rampant especially dysentery, fever and dropsy. In 1849, Parsonstown, for example, had the second-highest rate of death in the country where 756 people died and indeed in one week alone there were 101 reported deaths in the workhouse.[34] By 1851 the inability to bury people as quickly as they died in Tullamore became a matter of concern for Francis Berry who feared that this would lead to further disease. He reported to the board of guardians that Kilcruttin cemetery was so full that no more bodies could be interred without greatly endangering the health of the neighbourhood. In one corner more that 1,000 paupers were buried in the previous few years and according to returns for 1851 over 200 were buried in that year alone.[35] The board of guardians appealed to Lord Charleville to provide a suitable site for a new cemetery, which was subsequently granted.[36]

2. The Famine in Clonsast

On the eve of the Great Famine there were indications that all was not well within the Joly family, and indeed on their estate in King's County. In November 1843 there was evidence of the eviction of tenants when Joly noted in his personal diary that 'the Dooley's left their house after Mickey's death. It is now thrown down'. The following year John Plunket lamented the departure of his uncle's family to America to start a new life. On this occasion they celebrated their departure with a family dinner that included 'beef, ham and cold beef, plum pudding and apple pie'. It was a very different diet to that of the classes dependent almost entirely on potatoes.

Blight in the autumn of 1845 affected the Joly's crops and several days in late October were spent at Clonbullogue digging potatoes and turning out the damaged ones. Although the Jolys escaped the worst affects of the potato blight their parishioners were not so lucky. In January 1846 the daughter of an impoverished local family pleaded with Mary Joly for money, which was said to have caused the latter some distress. On another occasion a group of 'paupers', led by a man named Gorry, sought relief at Hollywood House, the Joly's home, in the middle of the night.[1] On this occasion Jasper and John Plunket accompanied their father armed with a gun, evidence that the people had resorted to desperate measures. Similar appeals were made to other landlords in the county: in 1846 Nicholas Biddulph at Rathrobin, near Ballyboy, was surrounded by several hundred starving tenants who demanded employment and who threatened to 'take food by force from wherever they can get it'.[2] In June 1846 the tenants at Clonsast dug the new potatoes early, probably because of the fear that they would be lost to blight.[3] In celebration there was an evening of 'dancing to the sweet music of Campion's flute' with Patsy Kelly, Tommy Corcoran and James Conlon playing other instruments.[4] But celebrations of thanksgiving were short lived. In September the late potatoes had to be dug quickly as 'the blast came on them so early'.[5] On this occasion Joly noted that 'the north wind brought the Dublin smoke' and that 'all the potato fields are yellow with the blossom of a fine crop of sharlocks'.[6] Likewise, Dr Cowell of Philipstown suggested that 'great rains and changes in the atmosphere' were responsible for the renewed blight.[7]

In 1845 on the Joly home farm a large variety of other crops were grown including cabbage, curled cale, cauliflower, orange and Belgian carrots, broccoli and Dutch turnips. Fruits included cantaloupe melon, peaches, pears and artichokes, which were said to have grown 'quite well'.[7] Moreover, the potato varieties they grew, such as the 'Bangor' and 'Oxford noble', were less affected by blight than the dreaded 'lumper'. It seems that the Jolys were interested in improving agricultural practices on their lands. Their huge library at Hollywood House indicated their interest in such agricultural practices as crop rotation and many books were dedicated to European agricultural techniques. The Jolys also chose to farm some tracts of land for themselves rather than sublet to a host of under tenants as many other landowners did. This practice was later championed in the late 1860s by the earl of Rosse and others.[9] Thus as the Famine worsened they encouraged the growing of other crops when the potato crop had failed. They were not alone in this matter. Indeed, there were some like James Devery at Cloghan who provided Swedish or common turnip seed and oats instead of potatoes to the tenants. Devery warned that although the potatoes looked healthy and promised a good yield 'so speedy is the change and so rapid its progress' one could not foretell the future.[10] By 1847, as table 1 shows, a variety of crops were grown in the parish of Clonsast including wheat, oats, barley, rye, beans, turnip and mangel wurzil. In particular there was a significant increase in the number of acres of turnips sown in 1847 compared to potatoes, evidence that the local population had been badly affected by the previous year's failure. The number of acres given to meadow and clover also suggested that large-scale grazing was favoured in Clonsast. Believing that local farmers could also be helped by agricultural instruction as well as relief, the Revd Joly enlisted the help of a Mr Cronly from Rathangan, Co. Kildare. Described as a 'teacher of land', Cronly instructed the local people both in dealing with the potato blight and in adopting new farming practices.[11] On other occasions seed potatoes were given to the poor or those adversely affected by the blight.[12]

Table 1. Agricultural returns showing the number of corn, beans and other crops (in acres) grown in Clonsast electoral division, 1847[13]

Crop	Acres	Crop	Acres	Crop	Acres
Wheat	928	Rye	31	Mangels	2
Oats	1238	Beans	40	Other green crops	98
Barley	69	Potatoes	244	Flax	4
Bere	57	Turnips	419	Meadow/clover	2592
				Total	**5722**

As mentioned before, in the county as a whole, there were many problems that hindered the provision of relief, including the petty squabbling between landlords and their representatives over boundaries and administration. In Geashill, Henry Norewood Trye reported that this lack of relief gave rise to the suffering of a 'miserable and mutinous' population.[14] However, Clonsast was rather exceptional in county terms and it was the organization of local relief there that spared the district the worst consequences of Famine. Although

2 The Jolys are awoken in the middle of the night by a group of tenants seeking relief, 1847

the Revd Dunne had clashed with Joly over tithes in previous years, they now worked tirelessly together in relieving the sick and the poor of the parish during the early years of the Famine. There had been a tradition of providing relief in the parish in the past, for example, during the cholera epidemic of 1832. In addition there were those who regularly provided shelter for the poor. In Clonbullogue there were 12 houses where shelter was provided for a small remittance.[15] In September 1846 Revd Joly and his son, Jasper, convened a meeting in Clonbullogue to raise subscriptions for the destitute of the parish.[16] They were joined by local Catholic clergy, the Revd Dunne, the Revd Ridgeway and other members of the parish vestry. This inter-denominational collaboration was also evident on 8 November when Dunne visited the Jolys at Hollywood House to discuss the plight of the people and was also present at St Kevin's Church of Ireland later in the month to hear the outcome of a vestry meeting.[17] Such collaboration may have been suggested by Joly's friend, Christopher Hamilton, agent of the Gifford and Tyrrell estates (which Jasper Robert Joly later inherited through marriage), who actively sought the assitance of the local Roman Catholic clergy during the Famine in maintaining 'some degree of social control on the estate'.[18] It was not until late January 1847 that Revd Henry Joly had to write to the relief commissioners at Dublin Castle seeking the rules and regulations for poor relief committees to organize the one which had just been formed in his parish.[19] Their efforts to raise subscriptions locally among landowners was successful and a relief store was opened and operated by the Jolys in Clonbullogue. Like other landowners, Joly believed that the burden of local relief should be shouldered by those who resided in the locality but unfortunately, there were a large number of absentee landlords like Downshire, Rosse and Downes whose contributions were minimal. Whether the measures adopted by Joly were successful or not remains unclear but by the following spring they sought the assistance of the central relief committee at Dublin Castle.

By 1848, landlords and agents who had been lenient to their tenantry now began to press for rents. The early years of the Famine had seen landlords and agents granting abatements of rent and encouraging certain tenants to improve their lot. However, after three years of Famine many began to change their management policies. Part of the reason for this change of attitude lay in the success of Repeal candidates in the general election of 1847. Landlords who had remitted rent or forgiven arrears resented the support given to the Repeal party. In 1848 the Repeal question dominated matters in Clonsast particularly among the tenants of the earl of Rosse in the townlands of Clonavoe and Colgagh. Rosse, it seems, through his agent George Heenan, was particularly adamant that tenants receiving relief should vote with their landlord and not the Repeal party. Tenants were forced to sign an anti-Repeal document in the presence of the agent. Previous to this, in February 1847, Rosse had introduced a set of 'estate rules' advising tenants how they should conduct themselves. These rules were probably introduced to avoid censure from newspapers and other sources when clearances and evictions were carried out.[20] The condemnation of landlords such as Mrs Gerrard in Co. Galway in 1846 proved that such 'rules' were necessary.[21] Between 1848 and 1853 Rosse carried out a number of clearances on his estates scattered throughout King's County.[22] In July an anonymous letter was published in the *Freeman's Journal* from a 'Clonbullogue man' criticizing both Rosse and Heenan for the publication of an anti-Repeal document. In particular the letter condemned the agent who was reported to have warned that 'whoever does not sign the document will mark the consequences'. In a jibe at Lord Rosse and his scientific endeavours at Birr Castle, the writer asked: 'how much certain loss will the country suffer if he neglect his telescope, and his attempts at discovering the whereabouts of the man in the moon'.[23]

As Famine conditions worsened in Clonsast, people sometimes resorted to crime. In 1848 the Jolys decided to erect new gates on all of their fields in order to protect crops and livestock. However, their attempts to prevent theft were not always entirely successful and in January 1847 Henry Joly and Peter Dempsey attended a fair at Mountmellick in an attempt to identify five of Joly's lambs that were stolen from Clonbullogue. The culprit, Johnny Brown, was later sentenced to six months imprisonment and was depicted in an illustration in the diaries being led away to prison with the caption: 'bad luck to auld dirty arse'.[24] That Brown had resorted to such measures was not surprising as the poor were said to be in a 'starving condition' despite whatever relief measures were in place. Public order was affected owing to the severity of the times and the continued blight of the potatoes. In August 1846 the police were called to a funeral in Clonbullogue where a fight had broken out among those in attendance. Poaching on local rivers was another problem for the police to deal with and was evidence of the plight of the people who tried to survive on fish. Indeed, even Joly himself was denied access to fishing on the River Figile and his nets seized when accompanied by the Ridgeways, Behans and Nelsons in July 1847.[25] According to local lore such was the plight of the people that several families including the Allens, Rourkes, Jones, Mooneys and Blands disappeared from Colgagh, Derryrobinson and Tronchoir in one week.[26] The Joly diaries also suggest that many people emigrated from the parish as conditions worsened. These included a Mr Poole who 'took leave' for America in October 1847 and John Campion, who 'bid farewell' in early 1848.[27] Another Famine victim was Kate Lawler whose 'putrid remains were found in a ditch near Capt Nelson's garden' during 'Black 47'. The social memory of the Famine in the parish also recalls that among the dead were two people whose corpses were found at 'Timmy's' cross in Clonsast.[28] In addition, as shown in appendix one, there were 38 burials at St Kevin's Church of Ireland in Clonbullogue between 1846 and 1850.

The diaries of John Plunket Joly show that his own family, neighbours and friends were not spared death during the Famine. In December 1846 Mrs Poole died from 'Famine fever', while in May 1847 Tom Behan drafted a will, believing that he was going to die.[29] Other references to death in the diaries include going to Mrs Nesbitt's funeral in May 1846, while later that month he noted that Pat Corcoran was buried.[30] Then in January 1848, his mother, Martha, died after several days' illness, surrounded by the Behans, Dempseys and Jenkinsons who had stayed up all night.[31] John Plunket thus described his mother's death:

> The Mrs breathed quick and drank spoonfuls of wine frequently till four o'clock p.m. Jasper being with her all day after which time she slept a few minutes and seemed quite easy and calm in her breathing which became slow and gradually weaker at ¼ before five when she awoke, fixed her eyes on Jasper and died, pleasantly calm. The Dr and Mary standing beside her bed, Jasper supporting her head.[32]

John Plunket accompanied Pat Redding to Rathangan to purchase deal boards to make his mother's coffin which was lined with flannel. A painting of his mother was also made so that a marble bust could be commissioned later. Family friends John Jenkinson Senior, Joe Cobb and Denis Dempsey dug and filled in the grave, while Peter Dempsey and William Hurst spread the sod.[33] Mrs Joly's death and burial was in stark contrast to that of the lower classes.

JOLY'S CLARE ESTATE

Conditions on Joly's estate at Carrigaholt and Killballyoan in Co. Clare were among the worst in Ireland during the Famine and were graphically depicted by the *Illustrated London News* in 1848–9. Located within the Kilrush union, by 1850 the population decreased by 17 per cent.[34] Joly's property, valued at £400 with 950 inhabitants, was located in the same barony as the Westby and Conygham estates, managed by the infamous land agent, Marcus Keane. L. Perry Curtis argues that evictions in Co. Clare took on a life of their own as agents vied with each other to see who could evict the most in the shortest space of time.[35] In particular, Keane, an 'exterminator general', managed 12 estates and was said to be 'unhappy when not exterminating'. He was so reviled for his actions during the Famine that his body was dug up and his coffin thrown outside the walls of the cemetery.[36] Ironically, on the eve of the Famine he was praised for his 'benevolent and humane character' by the parish priest of Carrigaholt, the Revd Malachi Duggan.[37] Perhaps hinting at the Revd Joly and others the *Limerick and Clare Examiner* condemned Keane's destructive handiwork as it was carried out for absentee landlords who were living in luxury elsewhere.

In March 1848 Joly sent a proposal to the Kilrush Board of Guardians concerning his tenants at Killballyoan. He wanted their support to send 150 'pauper' tenants to Quebec, Canada offering to cover two-thirds of the cost. However, Captain Kennedy, former secretary of the Devon Commission, lamented to the relief commissioners that Joly did not receive a single supporter at the meeting. Joly had argued that his tenants were perpetually in arrears, could pay no rent and when evicted would be left destitute to the world. He believed it would make more financial sense to have them emigrated, rather than impose extra costs on the workhouse.[38] The following month the guardians relented and accepted his plan, with Joly covering the entire cost, to be reimbursed by the union at a later date. The tenants sent to Quebec included 47 males under the age of 14; 22 under the age of 12; 50 females over 14 and 28 females under 14. In total it amounted to 147 people. The total cost of emigration including the provision of bedding, quilts and blankets was just over £750.[39] Those assisted in emigration by Joly were, it appears, the lucky ones. In June 1849 over 100 people died in one week in the barony, while in December, 41 people were drowned when taking a ferry from Kilrush where they had gone to the outdoor soup kitchens. They were reported to be making their way home to their 'wretched hovels' in Killballyoan.[40] Perhaps, surprisingly, when Jasper R. Joly married Maria Armit in January 1849 they chose to honeymoon in the barony of Moyarta on his father's Clare estate despite the obvious destitution prevalent there, raising the question as to whether the family were in touch with the reality of the Famine.[41]

THE SOCIAL WORLD OF THE JOLYS

By the early 1840s the Joly family enjoyed an affluent lifestyle and had established themselves among the landed elite of the barony. In 1841 Jasper was called to the bar and subsequently made a justice of the peace for King's County.[42] By this point much of the Revd Joly's time was pre-occupied with religious matters, including overseeing the business of the diocese of Killala, to which he was appointed as vicar general in 1839.[43] In 1843 Henry Revel was appointed curate at Clonsast to help Joly in his duties. His stay was brief and he was replaced by Thomas Dawson who officiated throughout the Famine years. Joly's youngest son, John Plunket, entered Trinity College in 1839 aged 13; received a BA in 1844 and later an MA in 1847. From an early age he had decided on a career in the church and his studies reflected this. He excelled in college life and revelled in the delights of Dublin and Trinity College.

Among their friends and neighbours were the Pooles of Clonsast, of whom William was the local constable; the Humes of Cloncrane and the Gatchells of Coolegagen, a Quaker family, one of whom (the aforementioned John) was shot dead in 1843.[44] They also included Joly's fellow clergymen in the neighbouring parishes: the Revd William Wakely in Ballyburley, the Revd Thomas Bell in Edenderry and the Revd Wingfield Digby in Geashill, while the Revd James Boyce, a relative, was the rector of Rathangan. Another learned family in the locality were the Ridgeways of Ballydermot House, one of whom, William (1858–1924), was later a celebrated Disney Professor of Archaeology at Cambridge University.[45] The Ridgeways were educated at Nutgrove School, Rathfarnham and were thus on the same educational and social footing as the Jolys. John Ridgeway was a keen poet with an interest in history and politics.[46] The Jolys often attended clerical meetings at Ballydermot and called regularly to dine and socialize with the family, exchanging books and conversing on social, political and spiritual matters.[47] It seems that the younger Jolys, particularly John Plunket, socialized with the Behans and Dempseys whose fathers were employed at Hollywood House and on the family's estate. Several entries in John Plunket's diaries refer to playing cards and draughts at Behans and painting 'Patrick's crosses' for the Behan girls. In May 1847, when Mrs Joly suffered a stroke, the Behans, along with the Dempseys and Ann Jenkinson, cared for her. Mrs Joly required round the clock supervision and night shifts were organized where volunteers 'lay on the car cushions on the floor with a frieze coat over' them. Indeed, Henry Dempsey was employed 'to keep the sheep from bleating within hearing distance of the Mrs'.[48]

To what extent did the Famine impact on the Jolys' social and family life? The diaries suggest very little. They continued with their daily leisure pursuits including chess, cards, skating, the flying of kites, fishing, swimming and canoeing on the local rivers. In 1847 John Plunket noted that they 'swam in a large deep swimming hole at Baly's Hill' and 'built a canoe and took it down the river'. Killanthomas wood, near Rathangan, was a favoured hunting ground where they shot wild fowl and buzzards and drank wine.[49] It is interesting that for the young Jolys, St Brochan's well and the ruins of Clonsast Church were an important feature in the local landscape and a place they frequently visited. They also continued to spend time visiting local castles and historic sites, sketching and making drawings of these. The diaries include sketches of Lea Castle, the cathedral at Kildare town and Carrick graveyard near Edenderry. Other excursions included a trip in June 1847 to Monasterevin to see the railroad works where John Plunket sampled 'cheese and cider', while the following month he visited Dublin Castle and then the Hibernian Academy to look at paintings on exhibition, later spending the evening at the Queen's Theatre.[50] The brothers also made frequent shopping trips to Dublin where they visited and purchased goods in shops such as Andrew's, Bewley's, Cranefield's, Piggot's and Pim's.[51] In July 1847, having paid and disputed for his MA degree, John Plunket bought a four key concert flute to celebrate.[52]

Music and dancing were the first loves of John Plunket and throughout the Famine he continued to play music and was the principal organizer of dances, recitals and other related activities. Social gatherings of the gentry were certainly not obliterated by the Famine and the evidence for Clonsast suggests that those who were fortunate enough to remain in employment also shared in such entertainment. In May 1846 a social event at Killahan when 'George Redding caused a dance to take place on the road, where Thomas Corcoran played the pipe and I the drum while three couples danced and the spectators shouted manfully' was well attended.[53] In September 1846 Joly noted how they had 'a march of flutes and drum from Berminghams to Behans, a party of Connacht men following us'; the latter perhaps looking for relief. The following day the crowds gathered again expecting to see 'some good dancing on the road, but as Chapman cut his fingers, he only had one round'. Another dance occurred the following evening at Behan's where 'Patsy Kelly and Julia Bean dancing to the music of Chapman's flute'.[54] In November they assembled for music in Clonbullogue as Joly beat the drum, while Henry and John Behan played the fiddle. Later the same month he noted that Johnny and Denis Dempsey were at Hollywood House where there was 'dancing and sport until 1a.m.'.[55] In January 1847, one of the worst months of the Great Famine owing to the severity of the weather, he notes that 'Henry, I and Natty Kelly played [music] along the road. In September 1847 after 36 loads of hay were drawn from Clonbullogue, Joly and others enjoyed an evening of 'lively entertainment' at which Ned Charmychael played the fiddle while John Connell and Patsy Kelly danced. Seldom does a day pass in the diary without some reference to music being played or talked about and sketches of musical activity predominate. Music was often provided by Joyce, a professional fiddler from Tullamore who travelled the county. Joly also refers to 'Nelson's servant man' who 'played the flute for me at Redding's'. The music enjoyed appears to have been in the main traditional airs. Despite the best efforts of Fr Matthew and the temperance movement, local musical gatherings and harvest work often resulted in the consumption of large amounts of alcohol. On one such

3 Music and dancing at Killahan, 1846

occasion, after the washing of sheep in the Figile river, Joly noted 'young Hanibo made sick by whiskey'. The Jolys themselves were not totally abstemious, and also drank wine they had made themselves after gathering, pressing and fermenting blackcurrants.

It was about this time that John Plunket was anxious to get a proper band master to come to Clonbullogue to teach those interested in playing instruments. He thus consulted with local men, Henry Farrell and Thomas Lewis, who both had an interest in music.[56] Farrell was a wealthy local miller and had a large collection of musical instruments including the clarinet, fiddle and violin. Dances were frequently held at Farrell's mill. By February 1847 Joly had employed John Delaney, a music master from Portarlington, at 10s. per month to teach certain locals how to play musical instruments and dance.[57] Delaney's lessons included dancing, particularly the polka, singing and lilting. Emphasizing that such musical gatherings were not open to all classes, in August 1847, Joly noted how Delaney taught 'a select group the first principles of polite dancing'.[58] Lessons usually took place at Hollywood House or at the police barrack at Clonbullogue, a favoured music centre for the young Jolys where they would beat the drum, while constables Lewis and Campion played. However, his conduct was not always exemplary and on one occasion Joly noted that 'he came here in the evening more drunk than sober'.[59] In addition to this Joly meticulously collected violin music from Delaney, the music master, and another man named John Low. It is, however, important to highlight that the money paid to such music masters by Joly could have been put to more effective use in reliving local poverty.

The Jolys also spent lavishly on other items. John Plunket was particularly fond of making things, including musical instruments, chairs, wardrobes, beds, tables and, most importantly, book shelves to hold his ever-expanding library. Among the instruments made was a drum with the inscription 'Eire go bragh-joy be with you' on it. The purchase of books was a weekly, if not daily, occurrence during the Famine and reflected his interests and advanced knowledge. These books included *The gardener's almanack, The vicar of Wakefield,* three volumes of the *Library of wilful knowledge on vegetable substances, Outlines of history* by Lardner and Smillis' *Philosophy of natural history.* The books were also enjoyed by visitors to the house, although the brothers kept a careful eye on their library. Hollywood House was also the venue during the Famine for the reading of newspapers and letters from emigrants. These included news from Denis Behan who kept in regular contact having emigrated in 1844. On other occasions they gathered at George Redding's for the reading of letters.[60] News of America and other places was also brought by return migration of Jack McGrattan who returned from America in August 1846.[61] A lover of nature, the Joly diaries also contain daily references and sketches of birds, animals, plants and insects. In April 1846 Joly was perturbed to find that people were robbing the bird's nests such was their predicament. Their condition was in stark contrast to the diet of his pet rabbits who were fed 'curled cale, boiled potatoes and sometimes a bunch of parsley, of which they are very fond'.[62]

Perhaps it was indicative of Joly's blindness to the suffering of the people in general that he noted in his diary the large gathering of people in December 1846 to 'slide on the ditch at Kit Cassidy's'. His perception was that the harsh winter conditions offered some form of sport, which of course hid the realities of life. However, the Jolys were not the only landlords in King's County leading comfortable lives and enjoying music and recreation during the Famine. In his memoirs William O'Connor Morris recalled that he had been left the owner of an 'embarrassed legacy' as a result of the Famine, lamenting that his family had done much to relieve the plight of their tenants despite not having the resources to do so.[63] Yet in January 1846 the *King's County Chronicle* reported on the lavish dinner which was hosted at the family home of Mount Pleasant to celebrate the coming of age of William himself. It was reported that upwards of 160 people enjoyed the dinner and 'a merry and well prolonged dance, in which our national character for fun was well kept up'.[64] A 'Ball and Supper' were celebrated at Tisaran, the home of Edmund L'Estrange, in August 1846, while in the same month Mr Armstrong of Balliver gave a picnic on a 'magnificent scale' at Strawberry Hill House.[65]

Likewise, in February 1847 a lavish dinner was celebrated and attended by upward of 150 people at Thomastown House for the coming of age of Francis Bennett.[66] Two years later the *Tipperary Vindicator* reported that whole districts of King's County were being cleared of smallholders and landless labourers

4 'At the barrack where Lewis and Campion played'

while Francis Bennett was hosting a feast for tenants on his estate, at which it was once again reported nothing was spared.[67] Elsewhere great festivities were celebrated on New Year's Day 1849 for Col. Westenra's tenants at Sharavogue at which the celebrated Cunningham the piper played.[68] The Downshire tenantry were regaled with music, dancing and festivities in September 1850 when the fourth marquis visited the estate.[69] At Birr Castle during the Famine it was noted that visitors enjoyed 'pretty good fishing' as there were large quantities of fish in the lakes.[70] In February 1851 Lord Rosse provided an extravagant display of fireworks for his tenants which included the wheel piece, roman candles, rockets and tourbillons. According to the *King's County Chronicle* 'no pains or expense was spared in their procurement', the final bill estimated to be in excess of £400.[71] The Ormond and King's County hunt continued to meet regularly during this period.[72] Race and hunt meets included those at Banagher in 1845; at Parsonstown in 1846 and 1850; at Ballymooney in 1846 and Tullamore when it was hosted at Ballykilmurray. In January 1849, under Mr Drought, the Ormond Hunt and King's County hunt met four times in ten days covering Woodfield, Ballyapple, Rathrobin and Glasshouse.[73] In March 1849 at a meeting of the hunt led by Col. Westenra at Golden Grove it was noted that 'not since the praties ceased to grow' had such a crowd assembled.[74]

Away at Trinity College John Plunkett's studies were undisturbed by the onset of Famine. These pleasant experiences included visiting his relations, the Barrys; taking long walks in and around the city with his companion, John O'Regan and frequenting book shops and libraries. In June 1846 he received an allowance from his father while he was also in receipt of a scholarship from the college, evidence of his outstanding academic ability. As the Famine intensified in July 1846 instead of returning to King's County the Joly brothers, John Plunkett, Jasper and Henry undertook a trip to Belgium, to the town of Charneux, in a quest to find out more about their ancestry. The journey via Holyhead, Liverpool, Birmingham, London and Ostend was marked by high dining and the boys indulged themselves at every opportunity. An example of their spending is shown below in table 2. Significantly, Joly records the plight of people on board who were emigrating to England; he noted that there were 'many Connacht people in the fore part of the ship and in among the pigs'. During the night 'a drunk bagpiper played and the people danced on the boat'. Many of these people, sick and hungry, were fleeing Ireland and John Plunket stayed up late 'looking at the sick people sprawled about the deck'. Meanwhile the Jolys feasted on beef, steak, cheese and cider. Arriving at Ostend they dined on 'soup, sole, beef, fowl, apple pie, egg pudding, cakes, gooseberrys, currants and a bottle of wine'. At Charneux, where their grandfather had been born, they ate 'bacon, eggs, potatoes, kidney beans, bread, cheese and ale'. Indeed the trip is littered with entries about the consumption of wine, ale, beer, cider and spirits. On one occasion Joly noted that 'we drank strong ale which, with the heat of the day, made Henry and I so stupid that we could not dine that evening'. In London they toured the city visiting St Paul's, Trafalgar Square, Nelson's pillar and a statue of the duke of Wellington. On the return trip they walked past Buckingham palace expecting to see the queen. At Charneux they obtained copies of the family's birth certificates and other documents in the town hall and visited relations, including a niece of his grandfathers, Madame Sharrat to whom Jasper gave '25 francs for which they were very grateful'. Arriving back in Dublin, the brothers set about buying presents for family and friends including a watch for 'Dinny' and a flute for Johnny Dempsey. When they reached Rathangan, Joly noted that they were met by the 'great smell from the rotting potato stalks everywhere'. Significantly, this is just one of a handful of comments about the Famine in the diaries.[75]

Table 2. Sample of the expenses incurred by John Plunket Joly on his journey to Ostend, July 1846

Item		Expense	
Night boat from Rathangan to Dublin		3s.	9d.
Fare from Howth to Liverpool		12s.	6d.
Breakfast		1s.	6d.
Rail from Liverpool to London	£1	7s.	4d.
Bread, cider & cheese			5d.
Fare from Ostend in the 'Rainbow'	£1	10s.	
Bill for 3 nights in the Bull & Mouth Hotel with servants	£7		
Dinner		1s.	2d.

The contrast could not have escaped him, so why was he so callous? The Famine it appears had no effect on him as he continued on his leisure trips. These included a visit to Kilrush, Co. Clare, by then a favoured holiday resort in Ireland and close to the family's estate at Carrigaholt.[76] This trip included a visit to Limerick where John Plunket sketched the town and stayed at the Clare hotel. He later visited Kilrush and Kilkee where he lodged with Mrs

Shannon and took long walks along the cliffs enjoying the scenery. Again the diaries offer no insight into the conditions or plight of the people of Clare, one of the worst affected counties during the Great Famine. Indeed, John Plunket did not even visit his father's tenantry in Clare; that job fell to Jasper, the eldest brother. Spending was not curtailed during the Famine and the brothers enjoyed many of the same pleasures they had done in previous years. Although, as highlighted earlier, the Jolys played an integral role in the provision of relief in the parish of Clonsast, more could have been done or at the very least their social and leisure pursuits curtailed.

3. Clonsast after the Famine

In June 1851 Charles Trench cleared over 700 tenants from the neighbouring Ashtown estate at Bracknagh. In social memory the clearances were said to have stemmed from a dispute. In 1850 Trench was said to have had a 'difference of opinion' with the local priest, the Revd John Dunne, over the building of a school in the parish. Trench commenced the building of a school at Bracknagh in 1845 and forced Catholic children to attend, bringing him into direct conflict with Dunne. When Dunne threatened to close the school a dispute resulted; Trench is reported to have said 'if Dunne closes my school then I'll close his church'.[1] In the 1930s the Irish folklore commission was told that:

> The landlord of Clonsast was Lord Ashtown. If a person got a new coat he would raise the rent. No man was allowed to sow the second crop with[out] manuring the ground or if he did he would be evicted. He built the Protestant school at Bracknagh, Clonsast and said that he would make the Catholic people go to that school and let their school go to waste. No person was allowed to sell a load of turf or if he was caught he would be put out of his house. He put Protestants into houses and the Catholics were put out and they had to go to the poor house or die by the roadside.[2]

Despite the obvious dislocation caused by the evictions in 1851 the event was not recorded in either local or national newspapers. In total 57 houses were demolished. It is interesting that a clearance of 700 people could have generated so little reaction. In his personal diaries, John Plunket Joly makes little reference to the clearance, except to note on 20 June that 'most of the houses of Bracknagh pulled down'.[3] The apparent lack of empathy with the plight of those affected by the clearances was probably as a result of the friendship between Trench and the Jolys; indeed the diaries record that the former was a regular visitor at Hollywood House.

The clearance formed part of new management policies on the estate that had begun in earnest two years previous when several tenants were encouraged to emigrate. In May 1849 Mary Dunne of Ballinowlarth gave up her holding and was given £10 for a passage to America. Others like John Kelly were evicted, while when William Coffey could no longer pay his rent, he was ejected and his holding subdivided among six neighbours at Bracknagh.[4] These policies were similar to what Ashtown's nephew, William Steuart Trench, would later undertake at the Digby estate at nearby Geashill in the late 1850s. Where leases, which had been granted for 21 years, had 'fallen in', the tenants were not reinstated and so a large-scale clearance could commence.[5] According to Ashtown several tenants came forward seeking assistance to leave for America and elsewhere. On the Joly estate, evidence exists, although not on the same scale, that they were also clearing their land of unviable tenants. In April 1851 Henry Joly threw down a house 'lately built by Nowlan' at Clonbullogue.[6]

By 1851 there were 5,667 uninhabited houses in King's County and the population had decreased by 34,000 people. Of these, over 15,000 had emigrated while 6,288 died in the workhouses.[7] The barony of Coolestown experienced the smallest decline in population (8 per cent) compared to the southern baronies of Ballyboy and Clonlisk which declined by 32 and 30 per cent respectively. There was a marked decline in population in several townlands in the parish of Clonsast. The townland of Aghameelick declined by 61 per cent; Bracknagh by 36 per cent; Clonmore by 35 per cent; Clonsast Lower by 32 per cent while the village of Clonbullogue declined by 50 per cent. In total there were 135 less houses in the parish after the Famine. There was other evidence of the social dislocation caused by the Famine. The number of Church of Ireland marriages in Clonsast remained low throughout the Famine – two in 1846; two in 1847; two in 1848–9 and four in 1850.[8] One of the latter marriages was John Behan and Joyce Watson, two of Joly's servants at Hollywood House who married on 12 February 1850. Despite the low marriage rate during the Famine, over 100 children were baptized in the parish from September 1845 to December 1851. These included three children born to Thomas Lewis, sub-constable of Clonbullogue and his wife Francis Sparrow.

Emigration continued in large numbers from 1851 to 1855. During this period 15,765 people emigrated from King's County, while a further 17,000 left by the end of the decade. Notably, it was lamented that the emigrants were generally the young and sturdy farmers, male and female and the families of the few remaining 'snug farmers'.[9] Some held out hope of return. Writing from Montreal, Canada, to his brother Samuel at Geashill, William Clay urged his family to 'be sure to clean up the rent, for I intend to see home again'.[10] The Jenkinsons of Clonsast were also among the exodus and left Ireland on board the ship *Olive Branch* in January 1850. John Jenkinson and his wife Ellen (née Short) had been married by the Revd Henry Joly in St Kevin's church in November 1834. Their 10-year-old daughter Jane was among the many Famine victims who died at sea on the trip to America. The Jenkinsons never forgot Clonsast. A newspaper report noting the 105th birthday of Ellen Jenkinson in 1913 highlighted that 'despite her advanced age [she] spends a large part of her time in singing songs she learned in Ireland, her native country, nearly a century ago. She says they are the best songs and that she doesn't care a rap about the present day songs'.[11] In Clonsast, despite the decline in population, many of the people mentioned in the Joly diaries

5 Revd Henry Joly checks Denis Behan's arrears before he emigrates to America

remained after the Famine. These included the Dempseys, Dunns, Cassidys and Behans. These were the better off who survived and benefited at the expense of others. Significantly, today, many of the names mentioned in the diaries of John Plunket Joly also survive in the area, including Blongs, Watsons, Dempseys and Cramptons. Although the diaries contain few examples of eviction or clearance on the Joly properties, that is not to say they did not occur. In June 1847 Joly included a rare entry when he noted that 'Henry and Dinny at Clonbullogue all day throwing down Murphy's old house'.[12] It is probable that there were others which John Plunket deemed unimportant to record.

Those who had survived the Famine were frequently in need of assistance. In November 1852 the Revd John Plunket Joly purchased blankets for the poor of Bracknagh and Clonbullogue, while the following year his wife, Julia, gave eighteen gowns and petticoats to poor women in the parish. John Plunket was also in charge of the dispensary at Clonbullogue, which his father had established during the Famine to treat various illnesses and disease. However, by March 1852 it was deemed unnecessary to keep the dispensary open and he brought home all the medicines. The early 1850s witnessed sporadic outbreaks of violence. In January 1852 he recorded in his diary that 'some evil minded rascal mutilated Henry's best ram by wantonly cutting away one of his testicles'. Such incidents had probably much to do with eviction and the continued failure of the potato which affected King's County as late as 1855. Walking the fields at Clonbrin in July 1851, Joly noted the extensive nature of the potato blight even though his own potatoes remained 'very fit to eat'. Later that summer he recorded 'the blight has appeared slightly in our garden and in a few fields near us but in general the potatoes look well'. On another occasion he noted that 'our potatoes look extremely luxuriant'. However, in the wider community there was renewed panic and the 'people are trying to save the harvest, the leaves are completely withered off the potato stalks everywhere'. In March 1852 he examined planting at Clonbullogue, Cloncrane and Bracknagh. The blight reappeared in the barony in 1853 and Joly's garden potatoes were among those found to be rotting.[13] As late as August 1855 Joly again lamented that the 'blight [is] back again'. As they had done over previous years, the Jolys experimented in growing new crops such as Aberdeen turnips and parsnips, while potatoes included seven different varieties with only one drill of the lumper potato planted per field. Joly was particularly pleased with the 'Scotch Downs' variety which produced good yields. A greenhouse was constructed by Pat Redding to cover peach, nectarine and other fruit trees, while covers for the turf clamps were also built.

The diaries of the early 1850s record Joly's attendance at a number of auctions of the contents of the houses of John Doran, Edward McEvoy and Christopher Hamilton, more than likely middlemen. During the Famine many landlords took the opportunity to get rid of middlemen from their estate who had long profited from long leases, many negotiated in prosperous times before the end of the Napoleonic War. These men were now deemed surplus to requirements and so, along with their host of under-tenants, were removed.[14] Significantly, they included John Abbott, who had acquired a new farm at Bracknagh when Ashtown carried out the clearances, but had quickly failed. Among the items Joly bought were round tables, a chest of drawers and a dinner table. Joly also attended the auction of landlords such as Lord Mayo's house at Palmerstown, Co. Kildare, and Castlemartin, near Kilcullen, Co. Kildare, the home of William Carter. The decline in fortunes of neighbouring towns and markets is also evident in the Jolys' decision to travel to Dublin for fairs where better prices for produce were guaranteed. On a number of occasions Henry Joly travelled to Dublin to sell his 'fat cattle' and wool. By now, like other farmers in the county, including Nesbitt, Bernard and Atkinson, Henry Joly appears to have moved into large-scale grazing in the period immediately after the Famine and he built several cow sheds in Clonbullogue for winter feeding. He was also interested in other economic ventures such as blasting the quarry at Clonad where men were put to work extracting the raw materials. This venture mirrored similar schemes of mining for lead at Blundell Hill, Edenderry and copper in the Slieve Bloom Mountains at Kinnitty.[15] The Edenderry scheme was undertaken by Lord Downshire and included over 60 tenants as shareholders.[16]

In the aftermath of the Famine John Plunket Joly appears to have been prospering as witnessed in his ability to lend money. Joly lent large sums of money to local people throughout the parish, as shown in appendix two. These people included Wilson, Cobbe, Powel and Goodwin and were among those who Joly called to see on a regular basis, possibly to prompt repayment. He was also in the position to lend £500 to Count Lusi, his father-in-law, although this appears to have strained their relationship: 'I trust never again to have money dealings with the Lusi family' wrote Joly in disgust.[17] Obviously he did not adhere to his grandfather's belief that you should 'never lend anything unless you are sure of being repaid'.[18] Joly's days, particularly prior to his marriage, were also spent visiting the sick, elderly and those affected by bereavement. In March 1852 Joly visited Mrs Haughton at Clongarrett, after he had seen her 'very unwell last Sunday' and requested Dr Dyas to examine her. On another occasion he went to see John Ward of Clonsast at 6.30 a.m. but was too late as he had already passed away. Others, like Simon Goodwin, were reprimanded for not seeking Joly's help and to say prayers when his sister Catherine died. The diaries for the early 1850s also record a significant number of deaths including several young people – George Tinckler, 'a fine boy aged 11', Samuel Moody, aged 11, and John Smith, aged 22, all of whom died in December 1851. The Jolys also experienced death at first hand. In July 1851, having spent weeks lingering with illness, Mary Joly begged her brother 'to crush her to death in my arms to end the miserable state she is in; half dead already'. Later that month he wrote: 'I fastened down the coffins and fixed the heart plate over the mortal remains of our dead and only sister. Henry and I carried out the body at 1 p.m. and placed it on the hearse … Henry and I and John Jenkinson and James Grady laid the coffin in the grave'. Mary's funeral was said to have been numerously attended and included family friends – the Jenkinsons, Dempseys and Behans. According to John Plunket, 'the poor archdeacon bore the melancholy ceremony with most praiseworthy fortitude'. Less than a year later, the Revd Henry Joly died after a long and protracted illness described as an 'enlargement of the liver and destruction of the right kidney'. About his death John Plunket wrote: 'The Dr is no more. No more about him except to try and imitate his good example by leading an industrious, useful, honest and truly religious life'.[19]

Although John Plunket was ordained in May 1849 in Chester, England, it was not until December 1851 that the Revd Henry Joly resigned the living of Clonsast and Ballinakill in favour of his son, which came with an annual salary of £460.[20] With mixed feelings about this period he wrote: 'so ends the month of June 1852, a month of memorable incidence to me. The early part of deeply clouded by the death of my poor dear father, my first and best friend – the remainder growing gradually brighter'.[21] Further evidence of Joly's growing prosperity was seen in the renovation of Hollywood House and of St Kevin's Church in the early 1850s. From June 1852 to March 1853 Pat Redding and Marty Dooley were employed to build new chimneys, knock internal walls, make new stairs, fit a new cistern to pump water into the house and new internal doors. An indication of the wealth accumulated by the Joly family was the dispersal of some £12,000 from the will of the late rector including shares in government bonds and a passenger ship. Improvements at St Kevin's also recommenced under his supervision, having being suspended throughout the Famine period. These included the planting of laurel and beech trees around the churchyard and the purchase of curtains and matting for the church. The number of staff also increased at Hollywood in the 1850s. Servants included Michael Watson, Catherine Watson, Martha Pattison and Sarah Jenkinson, while Mrs Dowdall from Dublin was employed as a nurse to the children. However, not all were successful in their endeavours and some like Jenkinson were dismissed 'having been impudent to the Mrs'.[22] In April 1854 Pattison was also dismissed because 'I could no longer allow her to remain with us, she is fond of being out with men'. Michael Watson was retained, although Joly must not have been happy with his brother's imprisonment for rape in 1855.[23]

The renovation of Hollywood House coincided with John Plunket's engagement to Julia (1827–86), daughter of Count Lusi. In May 1852, cupid and an arrow drawn in his diary indicated that Joly had found a potential wife. By now the worst years of the Famine were over. Joly's continued prosperity was reflected in the number of parties and balls which were held in their honour. At one such party there was 'tea, coffee, dancing, supper, courting, talking and fun kept up till 2a.m.'. Another party given by the Lusi family, at which there were 41 people present, was described as being 'very gay'. His uncle, Charles Joly also hosted a 'grand ball' where 65 people present were treated to a 'violin band, dancing, singing, courting and all kinds of pleasantry'. Afterwards John Plunket and the countess enjoyed a 'romantic drive in a covered car'. Preparing for his marriage he purchased a watch and chain valued at £21; an enamelled diamond ring for £4 4s.; a shirt and cravat and a violin bow. He also bought a grand piano at a cost of £42. Other purchases included frock coats, gloves, socks, a handkerchief and the usual collection of miscellaneous books and sheet music.

On 4 June 1853 Joly married Julia Lusi in a ceremony conducted by his cousin Augustas West, chancellor of Kildare. Having obtained permission from the archbishop to take leave of absence from his parish, the newly married couple, accompanied by the house maid, Martha Pattison, travelled to the lakes of Killarney on honeymoon. The couple stayed in the Victoria Hotel, rowed around the middle lake, saw Muckross Abbey, visited Innisfallen, O'Donahue's cascade, the Gap of Dunloe and Ross castle. When they returned to Hollywood some days later they were greeted by a large gathering of tenants and neighbours. Throughout the night there was 'great dancing around a bonfire', music and other entertainment.[24]

Determined to revive the spirits of his parishioners, Joly was responsible for the formation of a band at Bracknagh in the 1850s and purchased clarinets, cornets and flutes for the musicians. He also employed the services of a Mr Cronly as band master to teach them every Friday and Saturday evening for which he was paid £2 monthly, with the boys repaying Joly 2d. every month. In July 1856, 17 boys and Cronly played at Hollywood House 'all the evening' and were rewarded with tea, coffee, cakes and wine. Other social events resumed including the annual races at Clonshannon, tea parties, dances and musical recitals. One such recital involved Joly and Larry Farrell playing music at the old church of Ballinowlarth at 9 p.m. on a 'very fine night' in December. In 1900 the 'Joly band', established by John Plunket in 1851, was still in existence and numbered over 40 members.[25] Indeed music, song and dance continued to play a part in Clonsast after the Famine and the tradition of music at social gatherings such as 'saving the hay' continued long into the 20th century in the parish.

By 1857 and after only five years of active service to his parishioners, John Plunket Joly was in declining health. Despite receiving advice from several doctors to undertake a trip to Egypt or France for health reasons, he chose to remain in Ireland for the winter of 1857 and died the following March. By the 1870s his widow and children were living at 79 Wellington Road, Dublin and spent the months of July and August in a rented house in Greystones, Co. Wicklow. John Joly (1857–1933), 4th son of the Revd John Plunket Joly, was educated at Rathmines School under the direction of Dr Benson. His academic ability was evident at a young age and at 16 he had experimented with the construction of a thermometer, a microscope and a deep-sea sounding apparatus.[26] Later a physicist, geologist and engineer he has been described as 'Ireland's most eminent man of science in modern times'.[27] Henry Charles Joly inherited the King's County estates when his brother died in 1858.[28]

By the 1880s public antipathy towards the Jolys, at least in nationalist circles, increased owing largely to the memory of the Famine. Jasper Robert Joly irked local nationalists during the Land War when he remarked that Edenderry was a 'pestiferous' society and urged that a Defence Association should be established to protect their interests.[29] A land agent on several local estates, he was reviled by local land leaguers and was openly denounced at meetings in Edenderry and elsewhere.[30] A failed attempt to shoot Henry Charles Joly in August 1880 resulted from a grievance about evicted tenants.[31] During the revolutionary period, 1917–23, the Jolys were among a number of Protestant families who were threatened and intimidated in King's County.[32] In the midst of the 1918 Conscription crisis, the Revd Jasper Joly of Charneux House, Clonbullogue, confirmed this intimidation. Having been forced to sign the pledge against conscription under 'the threat of fire and sword' Joly added that 'a higher up Sinn Feiner came here with the list and threatened me that I would be treated just like the British soldiers they would be fighting against if I did not sign it, murder for me and my family and my place would be burned'.[33] In July 1921 Charneux House was raided by the IRA who commandeered bicycles, a car and furniture from his house.[34] Likewise, at Bracknagh, the Trench family were reviled for their role in the Famine clearances. The clearances lingered in social memory and the Ashtown estate was the scene of large scale cattle driving and intimidation during the so-called

In Memory of
JOHN PLUNKET JOLY,
YOUNGEST SON OF THE
VEN. ARCHDEACON JOLY,
FOR 6 YEARS THE GREATLY LOVED RECTOR OF THIS PARISH
BORN 1826 – DIED 1858.
AND OF HIS WIFE
JULIA ANNA MARIA,
DAUGHTER OF FREDERICK COUNT DE LUSI,
BORN 1827 – DIED 1886.

THIS TABLET IS ERECTED IN HUMBLE GRATITUDE BY THEIR LAST SURVIVING SON
JOHN JOLY, FELLOW OF TRINITY COLLEGE, DUBLIN.

6 Memorial plaque to John Plunket Joly in St Kevin's Church of Ireland, Clonbullogue

Ranch War and in the years prior to the War of Independence.[35] Such intimidation stemmed from the memory of the Famine and the wish of descendents of evicted tenants and others to be restored to their birthright.[36]

However, in 1929 when John Joly, then professor of Geology at Trinity College Dublin, visited Clonbullogue in an effort to determine his date of birth and the resting place of his father, the Revd John Plunket Joly, he was presented with an entirely different perspective. On this occasion he was accompanied by a member of the Scottish National Life Insurance Company as some doubt existed as to when exactly he was born. This doubt may present the reason why the diaries belonging to his father became separated and today remain in two different repositories. Finding proof of his birth (1 November 1857), Joly was informed by the then rector of Clonsast and Ballinakill, the Revd W.P. Connolly, that when his father died in March 1858 hundreds of people went to Kildare and carried the coffin all the way to Clonbullogue through the snow and ice. According to Connolly's account, they did so because they 'loved' and 'worshipped' his memory. Recalling his benevolence to the people of Clonsast, John Joly concluded by saying:

> There is no stone over his grave! I think of putting up one – but is not the love of his people the best testament to his memory? A monument raised in five short years of affectionate service to the poor of all creeds? Can any honour be greater than to be the son of such a father?[37]

Conclusion

The folklore of the parish of Clonsast portrays the landlord class during the Famine as alien and oppressive to their tenantry. According to Col. Eamon Broy, founder of the Broy Harriers and a commissioner of the Garda Siochána, local landlords and their agents had 'despotic control over the tenants' in Clonsast. For him, Clonsast was an area of good land, 'highly suitable for tillage, but cursed, as it were everywhere else in Ireland, by the blight of rack renting landlords with their agents, bailiffs and miscellaneous camp of followers'.[1] Whether Broy had the Jolys in mind or not is unclear, but as Peadar Mac Suibhne noted, when the Revd Dillon arrived in Clonbullogue, as parish priest in the early 1850s, he received a parcel of wild fowl as a gift from the Jolys. However, on learning from his parishioners about the Jolys, the priest returned the gift stating that he would not accept such from people who were evicting his parishioners.[2] Such perception of landlords grew from the way in which they were remembered as having treated their tenants during the Famine period.

This study of the Great Famine has been largely based on the existing diaries of John Plunket Joly. The diaries offer little commentary on Famine conditions or the plight of the people of Clonsast. Instead the diaries provide evidence of the lavish lifestyle and social world of John Plunket Joly and his family who frequently enjoyed social and leisure events, travelling widely, including a trip to Belgium in July 1846. By examining the social world of John Plunket Joly and his family it is clear that music, dance and other social events were not curtailed or disrupted by the Famine and contrasted greatly with the suffering of the poor. The Joly family continued to dine as they did before the calamity and there are only a few references in the diaries to them being directly affected by the blight. In August 1846 Joly noted 'we had bread for dinner for want of potatoes'. On another occasion he remarked that they had grated some rotten potatoes to make starch 'they being useless for food'.[3] The Joly family lived through the worst years of the Famine and managed, unlike so many of their neighbours and peers, to avoid the dreaded Incumbered Estates Court. Among these was William Poole whose estate was sold in January 1851 after James Smallman, the petitioner, brought a case before the Incumbered Estates Court as he was owed £1,948 or 11 times Poole's annual rental.[4] In King's County as many as 66 estates, or parts of them, were sold through the courts.

Naturally, it may be argued that more could have been done by the Jolys, particularly in light of the active social life they led and the fact that Hollywood

House was definitely a house of plenty in a time of want during the Great Famine. In particular, the £12,000 left by the Revd Henry Joly in his will in 1852 could have been used for the relief of local poverty, as could the countless sums spent on musical instruments, books, entertainment and refurbishments. Joly actually purchased several holdings during the Famine as the fortunes of others declined and these included part of the Purefoy estate and 'Casey's field'. Even during the worst months of the Famine, 'Black 47', the exterior of Hollywood House was painted, dashing applied and a gazebo erected at great expense.[5] Although it appeared that the Revd Henry Joly was endeavouring to alleviate the plight of his Co. Clare tenants by arranging for their passage to Canada in 1848, in many ways such schemes of assisted emigration were simply eviction by another name and relieved Joly of the long-term cost of providing for the maintenance of an impoverished tenantry. Other family members were also criticized for their role during the Famine. Henry Joly, a nephew of the Revd Joly, a solicitor by profession, acted as a receiver on a number of estates in Cos. Westmeath and Longford throughout the Famine. In 1849 he was accused of having neglected his duties by failing to press the tenants for rent or indeed provide assistance to their distress and poverty. Seeking his dismissal, Messrs Gale and Nugent believed that if he was left in the position any longer the estates would drift into ruin.[6]

Part of the reason why Clonsast, and by extension the barony of Coolestown, escaped the worst excesses of Famine lay in the effective administration of relief and the adoption of new agricultural methods in the years preceding the Famine. Relief efforts and the coming together of all the various participants including the Revd Henry Joly and his Catholic counterpart, the Revd John Dunne, were beneficial in relieving the effects of Famine locally. Relief efforts which had been implemented prior to the Famine appear to have been effective, while the operation of a dispensary reduced disease and illness. However, it must be highlighted that the efforts of Joly and others were often hampered by the large number of absentee proprietors within the parish who failed to contribute to relief. In addition, the failure of strong farmers to alleviate the plight of their cottier neighbours in King's County also added to the woes of the peasantry.[7] These strong farmers and those closest to the Joly family benefited by adopting new agricultural methods that had been championed by agriculturalists, agents and others. These new farming methods certainly helped alleviate the plight or at least reduce the devastation as experienced in other parts. In particular, the reduced dependence on the potato, the growing of other crops including wheat, barley, turnips, etc. and the sale of turf helped to relieve distress in the barony of Coolestown. Despite this the population of Clonsast declined by 25 per cent from 1841 to 1851, thereby questioning the effectiveness of the aforementioned relief measures.

   The Joly diaries provide an alternative insight into the life of the gentry in Famine-era Ireland. They provoke questions about how the Famine actually affected certain localities and people. How did local communities cope? Did life continue as normal or were some, like John Plunkett Joly, shielded or ignorant of the horrors around them? In many ways the diaries are interesting because of what they don't say as for what they do say. In particular, the diaries are remarkable for the paucity of references to hunger, death or Famine-related diseases. Indeed, even after a visit with Matt Goodwin to the Edenderry workhouse, where there were over 1,800 inmates in August 1847, Joly does not offer any insight into conditions or as to what he saw.[8] L. Perry Curtis Jr has argued that studies of the Famine are not complete without the horror stories of disease, death and the breakdown in surrounding norms when burying their dead.[9] Such descriptions of Famine conditions are in stark contrast to the foregoing account of the world of the Jolys. The question remains — had the Jolys become accustomed to death, starvation, disease and hunger among the lower classes by the time of the Famine? Certainly the Revd John Plunket Joly's sermons to his congregation during the early 1850s would suggest that he was aware of death, disease and suffering. Speaking to his congregation, Joly frequently referred to death which: 'has made us so familiar with it that we don't think of it. We see daily instances before our eyes of what we ourselves must come to, both young and old folk around us dying'.[10] While Clonsast may have been spared some of the horrors of Famine as experienced elsewhere, Joly makes no mention of distress in other places he visited including Clare and Dublin where he would surely have witnessed the devastation at first hand.

   Writing in 1993 James S. Donnelly Jr noted that historians must 'seek a fuller understanding of the degree to which [John] Mitchel's enormously effective charge' of genocide and race-murder against the British government and Irish landlords during the Famine 'corresponded to reality or illuminated it'.[11] This examination of the Joly diaries emphasizes the need to reappraise the Famine and the interpretations which have been reached in the recent past, particularly regarding the role of landlords. Undoubtedly, as more diaries and other such sources come to light in the future they will provide the potential to examine the issue of culpability during the Great Famine to a greater extent; an issue which has long been problematic in Irish historiography.

Appendices

Name	Date of Death	Age
Nancy Smith	9 Apr. 1846	67
Mary Leonard	26 Apr.	50
John Short	29 Apr.	61
Rebecca Johnson	8 May	78
Margaret Powell	10 Aug.	23
Thomas Adderly	10 Sept.	50
Thomas Smith	1 Oct.	66
Thomas Fairfax Eames	21 Nov.	97
Elizabeth Cobbe	13 Jan. 1847	30
John Lawton	15 Feb.	47
Margaret Tinkler	4 Apr.	3 months
Rebecca Smyth	19 Apr.	17
Richard Ward	12 Jun.	60
Isabella Ward	28 Jun.	97
Benjamin Lucas	27 Jul.	82
James Smith	15 Aug.	50
John Powell	13 Oct.	71
Rebecca Smith	10 Nov.	2 months
John Adderly	3 Jan. 1848	23
Martha Joly	21 Jan.	53
Francis Lamb	2 July	92
William Smith	27 Aug.	14 days
Harriet Moody	1 Dec.	3 months
Mary Anne Crampton	11 Mar. 1849	18
Isabella Ward	10 Apr.	16
William Adderly	27 Apr.	12
Elizabeth Moody	6 July	9
George Smith	4 Aug.	24
Samuel Crampton	19 Aug.	57
James Tinkler	4 Nov.	5 months
Rev Samuel Lucas	10 Jan. 1850	80
William Carroll	10 May	82
Thomas Brennan	24 Jun.	10
Joseph Ward	16 July	44
Samuel Hart	9 Aug.	2
Joyce Blong	6 Sept.	5
Andrew Tinkler	22 Sept.	2
Elizabeth Moody	23 Oct.	43

★ Clonsast Parish Records, 1803–98 (RCB Library P482).

APPENDIX 2. ACCOUNT OF MONEY LENT BY REVD JOHN PLUNKET JOLY
TO PARISHIONERS IN THE 1850s

Name & Residence	Sum lent £	s	d	When borrowed	When repaid
John Powel, Cushina	1	4	0	24 Dec. 1851	1 Sept. 1852
Do		2		4 May 1852	1 Sept. 1852
Charles Cobbe, Clonmore	1			10 May 1852	10 Oct. 1852
George Rea, Bracknagh	2			10 May 1852	1 May 1853
John Hynan, The Crook	1			15 May 1852	31 Oct. 1854
John Behan, Clonbullogue	1			3 June 1852	Nov. 1852
Thomas Wilson, Nahana	2			20 June 1852	10 Oct. 1852
J. Haughton, Cloncavan		8		13 July 1852	
George Rea, Bracknagh	3			15 Aug. 1852	15 Nov. 1853
Thomas Wilson	2			4 Dec. 1852	27 Feb. 1853
George Rea, Bracknagh	2			6 Dec. 1852	1 May 1853
Matt Goodwin, Cloncrane	10			10 Jan. 1853	Sept. 1853
George Rea, Bracknagh	6			25 Jan. 1853	
Charles Coobe, Violet Bank	1			14 Mar 1853	9 Oct. 1853
John Powel, Cushina	3	10		24 June 1853	1 Oct. 1853
Thomas Lewis	6			31 May 1853	Paid in instalments
George Rea	2				
Richard Lane	4				
Charles Cobbe	2			May 1854	
Mrs Lewis	2	15			Sept. 1854 £6 10s

APPENDIX 3. ARREARS DUE TO THE REVD HENRY JOLY AND RECEIVED
BY THE REVD JP JOLY IN 1852

Name	Amount		
Mr O'Donnell Co. Clare	£50		
Do	£16		
Cherub	£15		
Thomas Hume	£1	14s.	11d.
John & Chris Moody	£1	13s.	8d.
Gatchell	£66	11s.	8½d.
Gustavas Hume	£9		
Goodwin	£5	6s.	8½d.
Robert & William Moody	£3	7s.	4d.
Crampton & Pim	£3	3s.	5½d.
Phelps & Flanagan	£5	5s.	9d.
Co. Clare due by Poor Law Union	£27		

Notes

DP	Downshire papers
FJ	*Freemans Journal*
HC	House of Commons
Joly diary NLI	Diary of John Plunket Joly, 1843–48 (NLI, MS 17,035)
Joly diary TCD	Diary of Revd John Plunket Joly, 1851–58 (TCD, MS 2299/1–2)
JKAS	*Journal of the Kildare Archaeological Society*
KCC	*King's County Chronicle*
NAI	National Archives of Ireland
NLI	National Library of Ireland
OPKC	Outrage papers King's County, NAI
ORC	Offaly Research Centre, Tullamore
PRONI	Public Records Office of Northern Ireland
RCB	Representative Church Body Library, Dublin
RLFC	Relief Commission papers
TCD	Trinity College, Dublin

INTRODUCTION

1 Diary of John Plunkett Joly, 1843–48 (NLI, MS 17,035). [Hereafter cited as 'Joly diary NLI'].

2 Revd James Colgan, Edenderry to relief commissioners, 31 Mar. 1846 (NAI, RLFC, 3/1/1098).

3 *Correspondence relating to state of union workhouses in Ireland*, HC, 1847, [766] [790] [863] lv, p. 231.

4 William Wilde, *The beauties and antiquities of the Boyne and the Blackwater* (Dublin, 1849), pp 41–2.

5 T.P. O'Neill, 'The Famine in Offaly' in William Nolan and T.P. O'Neill (eds), *Offaly: history and society: interdisciplinary essays in the history of an Irish county* (Dublin, 1998), p. 681.

6 The papers are distinct from the Joly collection in the National Library of Ireland which contain 23,000 printed volumes, many unbound papers, prints as well as Irish and Scottish song music.

7 Patrick Henchy, 'The Joly family: Jasper Robert Joly and the National Library', *Irish University Review*, 7:2 (Autumn, 1977), 184–98.

8 Ibid.

9 C.J. Woods, 'Jasper Robert Joly' in *Dictionary of Irish biography* [accessed 7 November 2010].

10 Irish Times, 3 May 1976.

11 Henchy, 'The Joly family', 198.

12 'A volume containing typescript copies of pedigree and miscellaneous documents relating to the family of Joly from 1380 with biographical notes on individual members of the family, compiled by Jasper Joly, Dublin, 1969' (NLI, MS 16,524). [Hereafter Joly pedigree].

13 Joly pedigree.

14 This ceremony was conducted on 13 June 1774 at the King's Bench, Westminister.

15 Joly pedigree.

16 Frederick Fitzgerald, London to Lord Kildare, Carton, 15 July 1874 (PRONI, Leinster papers, D/3072/3/53/2).

17 In 1799 and 1800 he was promoted to second lieutenant and first lieutenant of the Stephens Green Infantry.

18 Elizabeth, countess of Fingall, *Seventy years young: memories of Elizabeth, countess of Fingall* (New York, 1939), p. 191.

19 Henchy, 'The Joly family', 189.

I. PRE-FAMINE LANDSCAPE AND
COMMUNITY

1 Sir Charles Coote, *Statistical survey of the
   King's County* (Dublin, 1801), p. 118.
2 Ibid., p. 121.
3 Donal Clarke, *Brown gold: a history of
   Bord na Mona and the Irish peat industry*
   (Dublin, 2010), pp 33–6.
4 *Slater's Directory*, 1846.
5 Thomas Lee, *Offaly through time and its
   townlands* (Dublin, 2009), p. 111.
6 Ibid., p. 125.
7 Conor McDermott, 'The prehistory of
   the Offaly peatlands' in Nolan and
   O'Neill (eds), *Offaly: history and society*,
   p. 19.
8 Clonbullogue ICA, *The life, the times, the
   people: Clonbullogue, Bracknagh and Walsh
   Island* (Tullamore, 1993), p. 16
9 Ibid.
10 Revd Martin Comerford, *Collections
   relating to the dioceses of Kildare and
   Leighlin* (3 vols, Dublin, 1883), ii, p. 124.
11 Michel Herity (ed.), *Ordnance Survey
   letters: Offaly* (Dublin, 2006), p. 27.
12 Elizabeth FitzPatrick, 'The early church
   in Offaly' in Nolan and O'Neill (eds),
   Offaly: history and society, p. 101.
13 Ibid., p. 103.
14 Ibid. See also *Leabhar Breac, facsimile
   edition* (Dublin, 1876), p. 212.
15 Caimin O'Brien, *Stories from a sacred
   landscape: Croghan Hill to Clonmacnoise*
   (Dublin, 2006), pp 199–200.
16 Lee, *Offaly through time*, p. 125.
17 'Copy, Letters Patent. Clonbullogue,
   Ballynowlan. Chas. II to Lt. Col. Wm.
   Purefoy, 29 Dec. 1666' (PRONI,
   D/671/D/6/2/1).
18 William Henry Milner, 'The
   Ballinowlart martyrs: local tradition in
   connection with the burning of the
   congregation in Ballinowlarth Church,
   Offaly', *JKAS*, 14:1 (1964–5), 41 and
   Revd M.P. Kennedy, 'The
   Ballinowlarth Martyrs', *JKAS*, 14:2
   (1966–7), 232–3.
19 *Irish Times*, 28 Sept. 1976.
20 'Clonbullogue' (MS notes, Local
   History Section, Edenderry Public
   Library).
21 Ciarán Reilly, *Edenderry, county Offaly
   and the Downshire estate 1790–1800*
   (Dublin, 2007), p. 36.
22 Coote, *Statistical survey*, pp 123–6.

23 *The life, the times*, pp 232–3.
24 'A survey and map of Clonbrin,
   Pollaghboy and part of Pollaghnecraige,
   in the parish of Clonbullock, barony of
   Coolestown, King's Co., the estate of
   the late John Walsh. By John Logan.
   Large folio sheet, coloured, Jan., 1837'
   (NLI, 16 I. 11 (6).
25 Arnold Horner, *Mapping Offaly in the
   early 19th century with an atlas of William
   Larkin's map of King's County, 1809* (Bray,
   2006), p. 7.
26 *Abstract of the answers and returns made
   pursuant to an act of the United
   Parliament, passed in the 55th year of the
   reign of His Late Majesty George the
   Third, intituled, 'An act to provide for
   taking an account of the population of
   Ireland, and for ascertaining the increase or
   diminution thereof'*, HC, 1824 (577), xxii,
   p. 82.
27 Thomas Murray to Lord Downshire, 20
   May 1839 (PRONI, D/671/ C/9/598).
28 Papers concerning the parish of
   Rathangan, its disunion from Clonsast
   and union with Clonbullock (PRONI,
   D/3078/1/9/5).
29 *Papers relating to the state of the
   Established Church of Ireland*, HC, 1820,
   ix.1 (93), pp 212.
30 *Returns to orders of the Honourable House
   of Commons, dated 10th July 1822, and
   26th February 1823; for accounts relating to
   the diocesan and parish schools in Ireland*,
   HC, 1823 (229), xvi, p. 31.
31 Quoted in T. Corcoran, 'Catholic
   diocesan action: the example of Kildare
   and Leighlin six score years ago', *Irish
   Monthly*, 63:739 (Jan. 1935), 26.
32 *FJ*, 21 Jan. 1845.
33 Michael Byrne, 'Tullamore: the growth
   process 1785–1841' in Nolan and
   O'Neill (eds), *Offaly: history and society*,
   p. 579.
34 George O'Brien, *The economic history of
   Ireland from the Union to the Famine*
   (London, 1921), p. 307.
35 Ibid., p. 317.
36 O'Neill, 'The Famine in Offaly', p. 684.
37 *Abstract of answers and returns under the
   Population Acts, 55 Geo. III. Chap.
   120. 3 Geo. IV. Chap. 5. 2 Geo. IV. Chap.
   30. 1 Will. IV. Chap. 19. Enumeration 1831*,
   HC, 1833 (634), xxxix, p. 57.
38 *Poor inquiry (Ireland). Appendix (C.)—
   Parts I. and II. Part I. Reports on the state
   of the poor, and on the charitable institutions*

in some of the principal towns; with
supplement containing answers to queries.
*Part II. Report on the city of Dublin, and
supplement containing answers to queries;
with addenda to appendix (A.), and
communications*, HC 1836 [35] [36] [37]
[38] [39] [40] [41] [42], lxii.i, p. 897.
39 Ridgeway papers (NLI, Ainsworth
Report on Special Collection No 284).
40 Coote, *Statistical survey*, p. 119.
41 Ibid., p. 118.
42 'Statement of Colonel Eamon Broy'
(NAI, Bureau of Military History
Statement, WS 1280).
43 Henry Brereton to John Ridgeway, 21
Oct. 1821 (NLI, MS 8833 (4).
44 *Aberdeen Journal*, 29 Dec. 1830.
45 OPKC, 1836.
46 Bernard Cummins, Kinnitty to Dublin
Castle, 19 Feb. 1836 (OPKC, 1836).
47 Ibid.
48 *Poor Inquiry*, appendix D, p. 23.
49 T.P. O'Neill, 'Cholera in Offaly in the
1830s', *Offaly Heritage*, 1 (2003), 96–107.
50 *Poor Inquiry*, p. 25.
51 Edward Wakefield, *An account of Ireland:
statistical and political* (2 vols, Dublin,
1812), ii, p. 686.
52 *Report from Her Majesty's Commissioners
of Inquiry into the state of the law and
practice in respect to the occupation of land
in Ireland*, HC 1845, [605] [606] xix.1,
57, p. 574.
53 *Poor inquiry*, appendix A, p. 897.
54 O'Neill, *Cholera in Offaly*, pp 96–107.
55 Diary of Charles Manners 1836 (TCD,
MS 11, 359 (1)).
56 Landowners of the barony of
Coolestown & Carbury to marquis of
Downshire, 18 Mar. 1820 (in private
possession).
57 Quoted in George Cornewall Lewis,
*On local disturbances in Ireland 1836 and
the Irish church question* (Cork, 1977),
p. 91.
59 *Poor inquiry*, appendix C, pp 1271–2.
60 Herity, *Ordnance survey letters Offaly*, p. 23.
61 J.S. Donnelly Jnr, *Captain Rock: Irish
agrarian rebellion of 1821–1824* (Cork,
2009), p. 124.
62 'Song for the 12th July 1843 by John D.
Frazer' (typescript, ORC).
63 *The Times*, 22 Sept. 1841.
64 *FJ*, 16 July 1842.
65 Neal Browne, Tullamore to lord
lieutenant, Dublin Castle, 30 Oct. 1844
(OPKC, 1844, 15/18245).

66 *FJ*, 26 Sept. 1845.
67 Ibid., 13 & 27 Dec. 1839.
68 'Notes on a repeal meeting held in the
chapel yard of Rahan in January 1843'
(OPKC, 1843)
69 Henry Quin, circular letter to Repeal
party members, 3 July 1843 (OPKC,
1843, 15/13607).
70 Lord Downshire to duke of Wellington,
9 Mar. 1841 (PRONI,
D671/C/12/777).
71 Rental of lands in Aughmilick and
Clonbrock, King's County, 1825
(PRONI, T/662 (105)).
72 *Nation*, 5 May 1843.
73 *FJ*, 8 May 1843.
74 Edenderry Family Lists Book (Quaker
Historical Library, Dublin, MM III
M1).
75 Lord Rosse to King's County
magistrates, 29 May 1843 (OPKC,
1843, 15/10377). See also Lord Rosse
to marquis of Downshire, 23 May 1843
(PRONI, D/671/C/12/842).
76 *The Nation*, 20 May 1843.
77 *FJ*, 20 May 1843.
78 Mr Despard to Edward Lucas, 13 May
1843 (OPKC, 1843).
79 Constable Archibald Johnson,
Clonbullock, to Richard Walshe, Sub-
Inspector, Edenderry, 20 May 1843
(OPKC, 1843)
80 Neal Browne to Under Secretary, 25
May 1844 (OPKC, 1844, 15/9013).
81 *Leinster Express*, 29 July 1843.
82 Jasper R. Joly, Hollywood, to under
secretary, Dublin Castle, 29 June 1843
(OPKC, 1843, 15/13193). See also *FJ*,
24 July 1843.
83 JR Joly, Hollywood, to under secretary,
Dublin Castle, 19 Sept. 1843 (OPKC,
1843, 15/18743).
84 Ciarán J. Reilly, 'Clearing the estates to
fill the workhouse: King's County land
agents and the Irish Poor Law Act,
1838' in Virginia Crossman and Peter
Gray (eds), *Poverty and welfare in Ireland
1838–1948* (Dublin, 2011), pp 145–62.
85 *FJ*, 24 July 1840.
86 Thomas Murray to Lord Downshire, 22
June 1834 (PRONI, D/671/C/9/455).
87 Helen Sheil, *Falling into wretchedness:
Ferbane in the 1830s* (Dublin, 1998),
p. 38.
88 *The Times*, 25 Dec. 1844.
89 Michael Beames 'The Ribbon
Societies: lower-class nationalism in

pre-famine Ireland', *Past and Present*, 97 (Nov, 1982), 128–9.

90 *Morning Chronicle*, 4 Dec. 1843.

91 *FJ*, 15 Apr. 1844.

92 'Address of Lord Rosse to the Parsonstown Agricultural Society, 1843' (typescript, ORC).

93 *FJ*, 23 Oct. 1845.

94 *The Times*, 27 Oct. 1845.

95 Joseph Grogan to Stewart and Kincaid, 16 Oct. 1845 (In private possession).

96 Joly diary NLI, 2 Oct. 1845.

97 Andrew Moore to relief commissioners, 20 Mar. 1846 (RLFC, 3/1/1055).

98 Revd James Colgan to relief commissioners, 31 Mar. 1846 (RLFC, 3/1/1098).

99 Thomas Byrne to J.P. Kennedy, 31 Mar. 1847 (RLFC 3/1/1095) and Michael Gilligan, secretary of the Coolestown Relief Committee to J.P. Kennedy, 11 Feb. 1847 (RLFC, 3/2/15/18).

1 *KCC*, 17 Oct. 1846.

2 Henry Sheane to William Stanley, 4 Nov. 1846 (RLFC, 2/441/41). See also O'Neill, 'The Famine in Offaly', p. 692.

3 Francis Berry to Lord Rosse, 21 Nov. 1845 (RLFC, 2/441/15).

4 O'Neill, 'The Famine in Offaly', p. 686.

5 Revd Henry Tyrrell to William Stanley, 13 Oct. 1846 (RLFC, 2/441/41).

6 *KCC*, 21 Oct. 1846.

7 Ibid., 2 Dec. 1846.

8 Francis Berry to Charles Brinsley Marlay, 5 Feb. 1847 (University of Nottingham, Marlay papers, MY 2467).

9 Henry Sheane to relief commmissioners, 23 July1846 (RLFC, 3/1/4653).

10 Enclosed in 'Neal Browne, resident magistrate, Tullamore to lord lieutenant, Dublin Castle, 25 Sept. 1846' (OPKC, 1846, 15/25911).

11 William O'Connor *Morris, Memories and thoughts of a life* (London, 1895), p. 88.

12 John Hussey Walsh to relief commissioners, 9 July 1846 (RLFC, 3/2/15/32).

13 *Correspondence explanatory of measures adopted by H.M. Government for relief of distress arising from failure of potato crop in Ireland*, HC 1846 [735] xxxvii. 41, p. 456.

14 Constabulary returns on the potato crop, 24 May 1846 (RLFC, 2/41/11).

15 *Correspondence explanatory of measures adopted*, p. 22.

16 *FJ*, 13 Jan. & 5 Feb. 1846.

17 Ibid., 25 Jan. 1847.

18 Ibid., 5 July 1847

19 *Correspondence explanatory of measures adopted*, p. 110.

20 Journal of James Dillon, King's County Coroner, 1846–53 (ORC).

21 *FJ*, 20 Aug. 1849.

22 *FJ*, 26 Oct. 1846.

23 *Correspondence relating to measures for relief of distress in Ireland (Board of Works Series), January-March 1847*, HC 1847 [764] lii.333, p. 23.

24 *Coms. of Public Works (Ireland), Fourteenth Report*, HC 1847 [762] xvii.457, p. 16.

25 *Return of Advance under 10 Vict., c.32.* HC. 1847–8 lvii.

26 John Julian, Parsonstown to under secretary, Dublin Castle, 20 Aug. 1850 (OPKC, 1850, 15/352).

27 See *A return of all murders that have been committed in Ireland since the 1st of January 1842*, HC 1846 (220) xxxv. 293 & *Correspondence relating to measures*, p. 110.

28 *Return by provinces and counties (compiled from returns made to the Inspector General, Royal Irish Constabulary) of cases of evictions which have come to the knowledge of the constabulary in each of the years 1849 to 1880 inclusive*, pp 3–23, HC 1881 (185) lxxvii, 725.

29 *House of Commons debates*, 1 & 5 Mar. 1849, vol. 103, c9 & 66.

30 In 1850, 270 families (1,516 people) were readmitted in King's County.

31 Sandra Robinson (ed.), *The diary of an Offaly schoolboy, 1858–59: William Davis* (Tullamore, 2010), p. xxx.

32 *FJ*, 28 May 1849.

33 *KCC*, 15 June & 10 Sept. 1849.

34 Minute Book of the Parsonstown Union, 1849 (Offaly County Library). See also O'Neill, 'The Famine in Offaly', p. 724.

35 *KCC*, 30 Jan. 1852.

36 Ibid., 16 Jan. 1851.

2. THE FAMINE IN CLONSAST

1 Joly diary NLI, 6 Jan. 1847.

2 Revd Andrew Shaw, *The history of Ballyboy, Kilcormac and Killoughy* (nd.), p. 126.

3 Joly diary NLI, 18 June 1846.
4 Ibid., 17 June 1846.
5 Ibid., 21 Sept. 1846.
6 Ibid., 20 Sept. 1846.
7 Dr J. Cowell to relief commissioners, 8 Nov. 1845 (RLFC, 2/Z15408).
8 Joly diary NLI, 17 Feb. 1847.
9 See Lord Rosse, *A few words on the relationship of landlord and tenant in Ireland* (London, 1867).
10 'Report on the inspection of the estate of Cloghan, King's County by the honourable Frederick Ponsonby for the Earl Fitzwilliam, June 1847' (NLI, MS 13,020).
11 Joly diary NLI, 24 Nov. 1846.
12 Joly diary NLI, 7 May 1846.
13 *Returns of agricultural produce in Ireland, in the year 1847*, HC 1847–48, lvii.1 [923], p. 38.
14 Henry Norewood Trye, secretary, Geashill relief committee to relief commissioners, 7 Nov. 1846 (RLFC, 3/2/15/ 29).
15 *Poor Inquiry*, p. 898.
16 Joly diary NLI, 5 Nov. 1846.
17 Ibid., 17 & 19 Jan. 1847.
18 Ballinderry papers (in private possession).
19 Revd Henry Joly, Hollywood, Rathangan to relief commissioners, Dublin Castle, 30 Jan. 1847 (RLFC, 3/2/15/17).
20 'Rules for the management of the Rosse estate' (Birr Castle Archives, J/3).
21 'Cases of tenantry eviction: letters and comments from newspapers, 1840–47' (NLI, 5A 3234).
22 See for example *FJ*, 22 Sept. 1849.
23 *FJ*, 11 July 1848.
24 Joly diary NLI, 2 Jan. 1847.
25 Joly diary NLI, 8 July 1847.
26 *The life, the times*, p. 3.
27 Ibid., 9 Oct. 1847.
28 *The life, the times*, p. 229.
29 Joly diary NLI, 15 May 1847.
30 Ibid., 4 & 27 May 1846.
31 Ibid., 17 Jan. 1848.
32 Ibid., 17 Jan. 1848.
33 Ibid., 22 Jan. 1848.
34 L. Perry Curtis Jr, *The depiction of eviction in Ireland, 1845–1910* (Dublin, 2011), p. 38.
35 Ibid.
36 Cathal Porteir, *Famine echoes* (Dublin, 1995), p. 222.
37 *FJ*, 25 June 1842.
38 *Papers relating to proceedings for relief of distress, and state of unions and workhouses in Ireland*, HC, 1847–8 [919] [955] [999] liv. 313, p. 800.
39 Ibid., p. 814.
40 *FJ*, 8 June & 17 Dec. 1849.
41 *FJ*, 12 Jan. 1849.
42 *FJ*, 16 Apr.1841.
43 *FJ*, 19 Nov. 1839.
44 *FJ*, 8 May 1843.
45 Ridgeway papers (NLI, MS 8833).
46 Ibid. (NLI, MS 8833 (3)).
47 'Letter of deacon's orders of John Powell, 1816, and a mandate from the bishop of Kildare to induct Powell to the rectory of Lea, Co. Laois, 1824' (RCB, MS 839).
48 Joly diary NLI, 30 May 1847.
49 Ibid., 8 Oct. 1845.
50 Ibid., 6 July 1847.
51 Ibid., 16 Nov. 1846.
52 Ibid., 6 July 1847.
53 Ibid., 8 May 1846.
54 Ibid., 1& 3 Sept. 1846.
55 Ibid., 25 Nov. 1846.
56 Ibid., 29 Nov. 1846.
57 Ibid., 1 Feb. 1847.
58 Ibid., 2 Aug. 1847.
59 Ibid., 22 Sept. 1847.
60 Ibid., 16 Aug. 1847.
61 Ibid., 9 Apr. 1846.
63 O'Connor Morris, *Memories*, p. 92.
64 *KCC*, 14 Jan. 1846.
65 Brendan Ryan, *The dear old town: a history of Ferbane in the 18th and 19th centuries* (Ferbane, 2002), p. 67.
66 *KCC*, 4 Feb. 1847.
67 *Tipperary Vindicator*, 5 Sept. 1849.
68 *Leinster Express*, 13 Jan. 1849.
69 *Belfast Newsletter*, 24 Sept. 1850.
70 A.P.W. Malcomson, *Calendar of the Rosse papers* (Dublin, 2008), p. 73.
71 *KCC*, 5 & 12 Feb. 1851.
72 *KCC*, 24 Mar. 1847.
73 *Nenagh Guardian*, 17 Jan. 1849.
74 Ibid., 10 Mar. 1849.
75 Ibid., 9 Aug. 1846.
76 Ignatius Murphy, *Before the Famine struck: life in west Clare, 1834–1845* (Dublin, 1996).

3. CLONSAST AFTER THE FAMINE

1 *The life, the times*, p. 270.
2 Quoted in Miriam Lambe, *A Tipperary landed estate: Castle Otway 1750–1853* (Dublin, 1998), p. 7.

3 Diary of Revd John Plunket Joly,
   1851–58 (TCD, MS 2299/1–2)
   [Hereafter cited as Joly diary TCD).
4 Rental of an estate in Clonsast, King's
   County, 1840–50 (NLI, MS 4337).
5 Trench papers (NLI, MS 2579).
6 Joly diary TCD, 19 Apr. 1851.
7 O'Neill, 'The Famine in Offaly',
   p. 701.
8 Clonsast parish records, 1846–1909
   (RCB).
9 *The Times*, 12 June 1852.
10 P. Frazer Simons, *Tenants no more: voices
   from an Irish townland 1811–1901 and the
   great migration to Australia and America*
   (Richmond, 1996), p. 72.
11 *Waukegan Sun*, 26 Dec. 1913.
12 Joly diary NLI, 5 June 1847.
13 Ibid., 16–24 July 1853.
14 See for example 'Journal of Michael
   Carey, Athy, Co. Kildare, including
   (indexed) copies of leases etc. but
   largely consisting of copies of letters to
   him from Charles Carey, 1840–1859'
   (NLI, MS 25,299).
15 John Locke, *Ireland's recovery* (London,
   1855), p. 79.
16 *Daily News*, 27 Mar. 1851.
17 Joly diary TCD, 15 Jan. 1856.
18 Joly pedigree.
19 Joly diary TCD, 7 June 1852.
20 *Liverpool Mercury*, 18 May 1849. See also
   Joly diary TCD, 11 Dec. 1851.
21 Ibid., 30 June 1852.
22 Ibid., 1 Nov. 1856
23 Ibid., 25 July 1855.
24 Ibid., 4–11 June 1853.
25 *The life, the times*, p. 288.
26 Diary and miscellaneous papers of
   John Joly, 1873 (TCD MS 11,180–
   11,180a/1–6).
27 John R. Nudds, 'The life and work of
   John Joly (1857–1933)', *Irish Journal of
   Earth Sciences*, 8:1 (1986), 81.

28 Diary of Henry Charles Joly, 1868
   (NLI, MS 17,035 (15)).
29 *Leinster Leader*, 12 Nov. 1881.
30 Ibid., 16 Jan. 1886.
31 *Carlisle Patriot*, 13 Aug. 1880.
32 Ciarán J. Reilly, 'The burning of
   country houses in Co. Offaly during
   the revolutionary period, 1920–3' in
   Terence Dooley and Christopher
   Ridgway (eds), *The Irish country house:
   its past, present and future* (Dublin, 2011),
   p. 117; 130.
33 'Revd Jasper Joly to Canon Jesson,
   1 May 1918' quoted in Peter Hart, *The
   IRA at War* (Oxford, 1998), p. 233.
34 *Leinster Leader*, 9 July 1920.
35 See for example John Noel McEvoy,
   'A study of the United Irish League in
   King's County 1899–1918' (MA thesis,
   St Patrick's College, Maynooth, 1992).
36 Reilly, 'The burning of country
   houses', p. 126.
37 Joly diary TCD.

CONCLUSION

1 'Statement of Colonel Eamon Broy'.
2 Peadar MacSuibhne, *Rath Iomghain:
   Rathangan* (Kildare, 1975), p. 50.
3 Ibid., 24 Aug. 1846.
4 *Daily News*, 20 Jan. 1851.
5 Ibid., 1 Sept. 1847.
6 *FJ*, 31 July 1849.
7 'Ballyboy petition' (OPKC, 1846).
8 Joly diary NLI, 18 Aug. 1847.
9 L. Perry Curtis Jr, *The depiction of
   eviction in Ireland 1845–1910* (Dublin,
   2011), p. 32.
10 Sermons of Revd John Plunket Joly
   (NLI, MS 8523).
11 James S. Donnelly Jr, 'The Great Famine
   and its interpreters, old and new', *History
   Ireland*, 1:3 (Autumn, 1993), 14.